ENGAGING MINDS
IN Science and Math Classrooms

Engaging Minds in the Classroom: The Surprising Power of Joy
by Michael F. Opitz and Michael P. Ford

Engaging Minds in English Language Arts Classrooms: The Surprising Power of Joy
by Mary Jo Fresch
edited by Michael F. Opitz and Michael P. Ford

Engaging Minds in Social Studies Classrooms: The Surprising Power of Joy
by James A. Erekson
edited by Michael F. Opitz and Michael P. Ford

ENGAGING MINDS
IN Science and Math Classrooms

Classrooms

THE SURPRISING POWER OF JOY

ERIC BRUNSELL
MICHELLE A. FLEMING

Edited by
Michael F. Opitz & Michael P. Ford

Alexandria, Virginia USA

1703 N. Beauregard St. • Alexandria, VA 22311–1714 USA
Phone: 800-933-2723 or 703-578-9600 • Fax: 703-575-5400
Website: www.ascd.org • E-mail: member@ascd.org
Author guidelines: www.ascd.org/write

Gene R. Carter, *Executive Director;* Richard Papale, *Acting Chief Program Development Officer;* Stefani Roth, *Interim Publisher;* Laura Lawson and Stefani Roth, *Acquisitions Editors;* Allison Scott, *Development Editor;* Julie Houtz, *Director, Book Editing & Production;* Darcie Russell, *Senior Associate Editor;* Georgia Park, *Senior Graphic Designer;* Mike Kalyan, *Production Manager;* Barton Matheson Willse & Worthington, *Typesetter;* Andrea Wilson, *Production Specialist*

Printed in the United States of America. Cover art © 2014 ASCD. ASCD publications present a variety of viewpoints. The views expressed or implied in this book should not be interpreted as official positions of the Association. All referenced trademarks are the property of their respective owners.

All web links in this book are correct as of the publication date below but may have become inactive or otherwise modified since that time. If you notice a deactivated or changed link, please e-mail books@ascd.org with the words "Link Update" in the subject line. In your message, please specify the web link, the book title, and the page number on which the link appears.

PAPERBACK ISBN: 978-1-4166-1726-6   ASCD product #113023   n2/14

Also available as an e-book (see Books in Print for the ISBNs).

Quantity discounts: 10–49 copies, 10%; 50 + copies, 15%; for 1,000 or more copies, call 800-933-2723, ext. 5634, or 703-575-5634. For desk copies: www.ascd.org/deskcopy

Library of Congress Cataloging-in-Publication Data

Brunsell, Eric, author.
  Engaging minds in science and math classrooms : the surprising power of joy / [authors] Eric Brunsell and Michelle A. Fleming ; [editors] Michael F. Opitz and Michael P. Ford.
     p. cm.
  Includes bibliographical references and index.
     ISBN 978-1-4166-1726-6 (pbk. : alk. paper) 1. Science—Study and teaching (Elementary) 2. Mathematics—Study and teaching (Elementary) 3. Science—Study and teaching (Middle school) 4. Mathematics—Study and teaching (Middle school) I. Fleming, Michelle A., author. II. Opitz, Michael F., editor. III. Ford, Michael P., editor. IV. Title.
     LB1585.B73 2014
     372.35'044—dc23
                                                                              2013043879

23 22 21 20 19 18 17 16 15 14   1 2 3 4 5 6 7 8 9 10 11 12

ENGAGING MINDS
in Science and Math Classrooms

THE SURPRISING POWER OF **JOY**

Acknowledgments

The following educators enriched this book by providing us with stories of the engaging and effective work that they do with their students every day—Jason Boss, Sandra Garbowicz and the teachers participating in the 13 grant, Patti Grayson, Harry Geiser, Darren Kellerby, Linda Kocian, Bruce Krueger, Ollie Schinkten, and Tim Sprain.

We would like to thank Mike Ford and Mike Opitz for inviting us to participate in this project. In addition, Lindsey Moses, Arizona State University, contributed teaching tips throughout this book to provide insight into supporting the learning of all students.

Finally, thank you to our families for adding joy to our lives—Emma, Sam, Melissa, Nathan, William, and Scott.

Introduction

*J*oy is one of those words that is hard to define, although we know it when we see it. *Joy* is a word heard occasionally in television commercials, but generally not in the course of our daily conversations. With the current emphasis on standardized testing, data, and accountability, joy is rarely part of the professional discourse in schools. But it is important, and joy in learning even more so. From kindergarten until graduation from high school, a child in the United States spends more than 11,000 hours in school. Over the same timespan, the average teacher will have spent more than 15,000 hours teaching. Can you imagine how dismal this would be if joy were completely absent from the classroom environment?

Thankfully, joy is not absent from our schools. We all have had joyful moments, as teachers and as students—magical times where things click, where you are in the zone, times where big smiles and excited chatter reveal an "aha!" moment of understanding. Eric fondly remembers his own experience as a student in a middle school science class, where the smallest person in class lifted the heaviest load using a pulley system and in which he learned about energy and power by sprinting up the stadium steps. Mr. Davis, the teacher, presented challenges to his students, who were expected to work together to figure out how to apply the science. Michelle sentimentally recalls her 9th grade algebra teacher, Mrs. Stephens, who provided multiple algebraic problems situated in real-life contexts and encouraged students to collaboratively work on solutions; she even used Carl Sagan's astronomy videos to illustrate her contention that "mathematics is the meaning of life!"

In *Engaging Minds in the Classroom: The Surprising Power of Joy* (2014), Michael Opitz and Michael Ford applied Vogt and Shearer's (2010) idea of *principled practice*—the consensus of experts coupled with professional experience—to create a framework for joyful teaching and learning that can be implemented in all content areas, including math and science. This framework comprises motivational generalizations, factors to assess and evaluate when creating a joyful learning environment, and areas in which to promote learning. As we reflect on the moments of joy that we have experienced as teachers and as students, it becomes obvious to us that these joyful learning components are inseparable. Teacher and students can together create a supportive community, activities can be playful and purposeful, and the learning environment can be content-rich and accessible.

In this book, we discuss how to implement the joyful learning framework in the science and mathematics classroom. In Chapter 1, we explore the definition of joyful teaching and learning, specifically as it applies to teaching math and science. This discussion incorporates both evidence from educational research and our own beliefs, based on our professional experience, regarding engagement and motivation.

In Chapter 2, we discuss five elements that can help teachers maximize the benefits of joyful teaching and learning:

- Understanding students as learners,
- Understanding ourselves as teachers,
- Evaluating the relevance of the text and materials we use,
- Determining how assessments can help us improve practice, and
- Understanding how schoolwide configurations influence student learning.

In Chapter 3, the rubber hits the road: we provide a framework for implementing joyful teaching and learning and examples of the framework in action, in mathematics and science activities.

In Chapter 4, we address how the framework for joyful teaching and learning relates to contemporary education initiatives such as Response to

Intervention, the Common Core State Standards, and the Next Generation Science Standards. Another concern for many teachers is how to connect with diverse students, particularly English language learners (ELLs). This is also a focus of the *Engaging Minds in the Classroom* series, so throughout this book, we include teaching tips that suggest specific strategies and highlight research on how to support ELLs in science and math.

Joyful teaching and learning experiences are often described as *magical*. But, as Arthur C. Clarke has been widely quoted as noting, "Magic is just science that we don't understand yet." Our hope is that this book will help you develop an understanding of joyful teaching and learning in science and mathematics. To echo Opitz and Ford (2014),

> We want to help you uncover ways to take this information and apply it to your own unique teaching experience.
>
> Fortunately, this information will fit into your existing classroom routines; much of it is more about your mindset about learners, content, and teaching than it is about adding new content to your already overstuffed curricula. (p. 4)

Our goal is to help you create those magical moments on a regular basis. Because, as author Sidney Sheldon states, "There is magic, but you have to be the magician. You have to make the magic happen" (2004, p. 52).

CHAPTER 1

Understanding Joyful Learning in Science and Math

One of Eric's students once said, "That was a fun class, but I learned a lot, too." For students, fun and learning often seem mutually exclusive. Is there something about learning that excludes the possibility that it could be fun? We hope not! However, for learning to occur, something deeper has to happen than students just having fun: they need to be motivated and engaged in the learning process.

Defining Joyful Learning

Opitz and Ford (2014) defined *joyful learning* as "acquiring knowledge or skills in ways that cause pleasure and happiness" (p. 10). The joyful learning process requires and builds on noncognitive skills as well as academic knowledge. Skills such as resilience, persistence, determination, and willingness to problem solve lay the foundation for joy in learning. Basically, when students are engaged learners, joy emanates from success in the learning process (Rantala & Maatta, 2012; Tough, 2012).

A Joyful Learning Framework

Opitz and Ford's (2014) review of the research and reflection on their own experiences led them to conclude that joy has *everything* to do with learning. What also became clear is that understanding why joyful learning

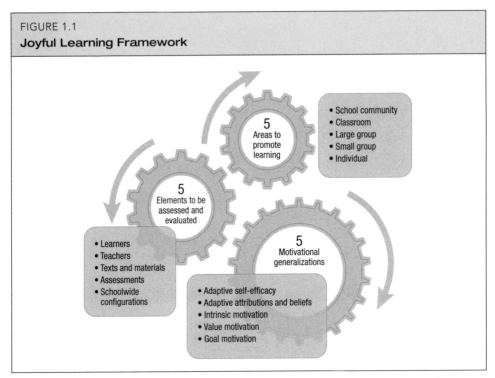

FIGURE 1.1
Joyful Learning Framework

5 Areas to promote learning
- School community
- Classroom
- Large group
- Small group
- Individual

5 Elements to be assessed and evaluated
- Learners
- Teachers
- Texts and materials
- Assessments
- Schoolwide configurations

5 Motivational generalizations
- Adaptive self-efficacy
- Adaptive attributions and beliefs
- Intrinsic motivation
- Value motivation
- Goal motivation

Source: From *Engaging Minds in the Classroom: The Surprising Power of Joy* (p. 14), by M. F. Opitz and M. P. Ford, 2014, Alexandria, VA: ASCD. © 2014 ASCD. Reprinted with permission.

is so important left questions about how to implement it unanswered. They saw the need to create a framework that would help teachers make decisions about joyful learning more systematic, intentional, and purposeful. The resulting framework consists of three parts (see Figure 1.1):

1. Five motivational generalizations: adaptive self-efficacy and competence beliefs, adaptive attributions and beliefs about control, higher levels of interest and intrinsic motivation, higher levels of value, and goals.

2. Five elements that need to be assessed and evaluated in order to get the most from joyful learning: learners, teachers, texts and materials, assessments, and schoolwide configurations.

3. Five key areas in which to promote joyful learning: school community, physical environment, whole-group instruction, small-group instruction, and individual instruction.

This framework is the basis for planning and teaching and learning, to which we have applied our own research and experience in teaching math and science. To offer a practical extension of joyful learning, we also identify teaching activities in each of the five areas that are compatible with what we have learned (see Chapter 3), to illustrate how the framework comes to life in a classroom.

Motivation, Engagement, and Joy in Mathematics and Science

Joyful learning is strongly connected to "better" learning. In a recent study of middle school science students, Liu, Horton, Olmanson, and Toprac (2011) found a quantifiable relationship between student enjoyment of an activity and increases in content knowledge. Similarly, factors related to joyful learning are also critical to learning elementary and middle school mathematics (Schweinle, Meyer, & Turner, 2006).

Opitz and Ford (2014) suggest that joyful learning begins with students who are motivated and engaged. Factors that influence motivation include self-efficacy and competence beliefs, attributions and control beliefs, interest and intrinsic motivation, perceptions of value, and goal orientation (see Figure 1.2). *Self-efficacy* is a measure of students' confidence in their ability to master a new skill, task, or content. Self-efficacy in one domain (e.g., science) can be different from the student's self-efficacy in another domain (e.g., math).

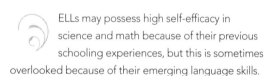

ELLs may possess high self-efficacy in science and math because of their previous schooling experiences, but this is sometimes overlooked because of their emerging language skills.

Engagement—being attentive, committed, persistent, and seeking meaning—is closely related to motivation and often seen as the visible outcome of motivation. A five-year National Science Foundation (NSF) project (Fast et al., 2010) focusing on upper elementary mathematics found that many of the factors related to motivation and engagement are intertwined and have a positive influence on student achievement:

FIGURE 1.2
Generalizations About Motivation, and Instructional Implications

Generalization	Description	Instructional Implication
Adaptive self-efficacy and competence beliefs motivate students.	*Self-efficacy* focuses on judgment about one's ability to successfully perform a general task ("I'm good at math") or a specific given task ("I'm very good at solving story problems"). *Competence* beliefs focus on how well a person expects to perform ("I can do this").	• Provide clear and accurate feedback regarding self-efficacy and competence and focus on students' developing competence, expertise, and skill. • Design tasks that challenge students yet provide opportunities for success. • Involve students in monitoring their progress and growth so they can discover insights about themselves as learners.
Adaptive attributions and control beliefs motivate students.	*Attributions* and *control beliefs* are to beliefs about what might cause success or failure with a given task and the degree of control one has over attaining the learning at hand. For example, "If I think deeper about this and make a greater effort, I will be able to do this" versus "I'm not as lucky as my friend who got this right."	• Provide feedback that emphasizes learning process, including the importance of effort, strategies, and self-control. • Provide strategy instruction that goes beyond declarative knowledge (what) and includes procedural (how) and conditional (why and when) knowledge as well. • Use language that focuses on controllable aspects of learning (effort, ways of thinking, strategy knowledge) and redirect language that focuses on uncontrollable aspects (luck, genes, other people's behavior). • Share examples of how "failure" is a natural part of the ultimate successful efforts. Let learners know "if at first you don't succeed, join the club!"
Higher levels of interest and intrinsic motivation motivate students.	*Value* is the importance that an individual associates with a task. *Intrinsic value* (see Wigfield and Eccles, 2002) is the enjoyment or interest the learner experiences when completing a given activity ("I can't wait to find the time so I can finish reading the next book in this series").	• Use assessment surveys that allow for insights about and across students in terms of their interests in topics, learning methods, and materials. • Provide stimulating and interesting activities that incorporate many different materials. • Provide a variety of activities, some of which are unique. • Provide content and tasks that are meaningful to students. • Show interest and involvement in the content and activities. • Allow for choice in the selection of activities, content, and materials.

FIGURE 1.2

Generalizations About Motivation, and Instructional Implications *(continued)*

Generalization	Description	Instructional Implication
Higher levels of value motivate students.	Other forms of value are attainment, utility, and cost (Wigfield & Eccles, 2002). *Attainment* is the importance the learner attaches to doing well on the task. *Utility* is how useful the task is to achieving a future goal ("I want to do well on this essay because I want to post it on the school website"). *Cost* is perception of the activity in terms of time and effort ("This will be a helpful way to review and it won't take a bunch of time").	• Use assessment surveys that allow for insights about and across students in terms of short-term goals, long-term goals, and current behaviors related to school work. • Provide tasks, material, and activities that are relevant and useful to students and allow for some personal identification. • Discuss with students the importance and utility of the content they are learning and the activities they complete. Help them to understand why they are doing what they are doing.
Goals motivate and direct students.	*Goal content*, which focuses on establishing something to attain, and *goal orientation*, which focuses on the purpose or reason for engaging in an activity, are two important parts to consider when thinking about goals. *Mastery-goal orientation* encourages students to approach the task in order to learn it well and gain new competence. *Performance goal orientation* leads one to demonstrate ability for others to seek reward or recognition (Rueda, 2011).	• Use organizational and management structures that encourage personal and social responsibility including the setting of personal and classwide goals. • Provide a safe, comfortable, and predictable environment. • Use cooperative and collaborative groups to afford students with opportunities to attain both social and academic goals. • Discuss with students the importance of mastering learning and understanding course and lesson content. • Use task, reward, and evaluation structures that promote mastery, learning, effort, progress, and self-improvement standards and deemphasize social comparison or norm-referenced standards.

Source: From *Engaging Minds in the Classroom: The Surprising Power of Joy* (p. 12–13), by M. F. Opitz and M. P. Ford, 2014, Alexandria, VA: ASCD. © 2014 ASCD. Reprinted with permission.

> Students who perceived their classroom environments as more car-
> ing, challenging, and mastery-oriented classrooms had significantly
> higher levels of math self-efficacy than those in less caring, chal-
> lenging, and mastery-oriented classrooms. In addition, we found
> that higher levels of math self-efficacy positively affected student
> math performance. (p. 736)

The NSF researchers found that "perceptions of the classroom environment indirectly affect math performance through self-efficacy [suggesting] that what teachers do in the classroom matters" (p. 738). Pintrich, Marx, and Boyle (1993) had also noted much earlier that students' motivational beliefs about themselves as learners (i.e., interests, goals, values, self-efficacy, and control beliefs) play an important role in science learning.

Implications for Teaching Science and Mathematics

The way that you approach teaching mathematics and science influences students' motivation, engagement, and self-efficacy. Understanding how to build on students' personal interests or generate situational interest can help you create a classroom culture where students' learning goals are focused on understanding concepts. Students' perception of the challenge of a learning task also affects their motivation, so we will discuss how you can minimize math anxiety.

Establishing content and language objectives, scaffolding language, and using comprehensible input are all strategies that can support ELL acquisition of math and science concepts.

In addition, teacher feedback and student self-reflection (*metacognition*) can enhance self-efficacy and other affective factors.

Build on Student Interest

Andre and Widschitl (2003) described interest as either personal or situational. *Personal interest* is interest that occurs outside the classroom. *Situational interest* is generated within a specific classroom context (e.g., using a "hook" during instruction). Instruction that focuses on essential questions related to students' lives and authentic concerns increases student interest. In addition, providing opportunities for dialogue and sense making during class (as opposed to the unproblematic absorbing of information), using multiple representations of concepts, and allowing students to express their understanding using a variety of modes increase student interest.

> The day after his 8th grade science students learn that bacteria would not grow in small areas around certain spices, Alex Martinez engages them in a sense-making activity. He starts class with the prompt "Cultures in warmer climates tend to cook with more spices than those in cold climates. Researchers also found that meat dishes use more spices than vegetable dishes. Why do you think this is the case?" Students discuss this in small groups and then write arguments that include a claim and supporting evidence. Although they do not yet use the scientific vocabulary, Mr. Martinez's students in effect use evidence from the laboratory to explain the concept of a zone of inhibition.

Focus on Mastery Goals

Although students' goals related to learning are multifaceted, they can generally be classified as either a *mastery* goal or a *performance* goal. Students as a group exhibit characteristics of both orientations, with individuals leaning more strongly in one direction than the other. Students who lean toward a mastery-goal orientation focus on learning and understanding content; they care more about understanding the topic than the grade they receive. Students with a performance-goal orientation focus on demonstrating their ability relative to others; they want an *A*, but don't really care if they understand the content. Linnenbrink and Pintrich (2003) found that students with mastery-goal orientation show greater science learning gains than those with a performance-goal orientation. Similar findings have been found in learning mathematics (Blackwell, Trzesniewski, & Dweck, 2007).

To promote mastery goals, emphasize learning and create situations where students can make choices and feel autonomous. Recognizing students for improvement also can help promote the adoption of mastery goals. Classrooms where teachers use normative grading and recognize students or their performance relative to others promote performance goals (Linnenbrink & Pintrich, 2003).

> Tanya Schaffer challenges her 6th grade students to apply their understanding of mathematics to an authentic task from the website Math by Design—and her lesson incorporates choice and autonomy. Students can work individually or in small groups. They can choose between the website's two projects: designing a community park or an environmental center. Because the tasks involved in the scenarios do not have obvious solution pathways, students also have to choose how to solve the tasks. At the conclusion, Ms. Schaffer's students respond to a series of questions that focus on the mathematical concepts underlying their decisions. With this project, Ms. Schaffer effectively promotes her students' mastery goals, keeping the emphasis on their learning and progress over getting a "correct" answer.

Establish Appropriate Level of Challenge

A rewarding activity in math or science needs to be at an appropriate difficulty level so that students perceive that they have the skills to accomplish it. Students can quickly become unmotivated and disengaged if the challenge level and skill level are out of balance (Csikszentmihalyi & Nakamura, 1989). Schweinle and colleagues (2006) found that elementary students often perceive more challenging math problems as threatening, which can lead to decreased self-efficacy and increased math anxiety. O'Donnell's review of common practices among successful mathematics teachers (2009) provided a series of tips for helping students approach challenging mathematics activities. Her findings included activities that reinforce mastery, such as having students clarify their ideas, and asking questions that prompt deeper understanding; having students distill others' ideas or explanations; offering different representations of concepts; and embedding time in the lesson to allow students to digest new information or formulate ideas.

> Sandra Kim has noticed that some students in her combined 2nd/3rd grade are struggling with the concept of regrouping during subtraction and addition problems and becoming frustrated.

To allow students to use different representations of the problem and explore their own reasoning and that of their classmates, she introduces a "banking" activity. She gives some students (the "bankers") full sets of manipulatives consisting of multiple flats (equivalent to 100 blocks), rods (equivalent to 10 blocks), and individual blocks. The remaining students are paired up; one student from each pair has two rods and a flat (value: 120 blocks). Ms. Kim instructs these students to give their partners exactly 35 blocks. When they complain that it is not possible, she acts surprised: "But don't you have 120? Why can't you give your partner 35?"

> To support ELL acquisition of concepts and avoid anxiety, provide additional wait time for processing and translation, present essential academic vocabulary, and offer visual representations and manipulatives.

She displays the problem (120 − 35) on an interactive whiteboard, which also includes images of base-10 blocks. The pairs of students work with bankers to make exchanges that will allow them to subtract the correct number of blocks; Ms. Kim shows the regrouping on the board, using both numbers and the virtual manipulatives. After successfully completing the transaction, students rotate roles and start a new problem. At the end of the activity, she leads a class discussion that explicitly connects the work of the banker to the process of regrouping during addition and subtraction.

Incorporate Feedback and Self-Reflection

Schweinle and colleagues (2006) found that "when [teacher] feedback was frequent, elaborative, positive, and used to help students develop understanding . . . students reported higher affect, efficacy, and importance"; but "when feedback was minimal or when it appeared to be evaluative, students expressed less positive motivation and affect" (p. 288). Similarly, self-reflection leads to deeper understanding, mastery-goal orientation, and stronger self-regulating behaviors. In a study involving 5th grade students' science learning, Georghiades (2000) found that students engaging in brief self-reflective (metacognitive) instances at selected points during

Encourage ELLs in metacognitive activities related to the language needed to construct meaning about the given topic and participate in meaningful discussions. Consider both basic interpersonal communicative skills (BICS) and cognitive academic language proficiency (CALP).

instruction were more engaged and remembered more of the taught material. Activities included participating in questions and discussions about beliefs before and after lessons, explaining their thinking in approaching a problem to each other, keeping a diary of new concepts, and preparing graphic representations (e.g., annotated drawings, concept maps).

Interactive notebooks have become a popular tool in science classrooms (see the website Science Spot for links, http://sciencespot.net/Pages /ISNinfo.html). We have worked with teachers across all grade levels to integrate the use of interactive science notebooks, using a format that specifically focuses student reflection on their learning (Marcarelli, 2010). Students use the right-hand side of their notebook for writing notes, recording data, or keeping track of other inputs; the left-hand side is reserved for student reflection and meaning making. On this page, students respond to teacher prompts that ask them to synthesize information, describe how an activity changed their thinking about a topic, or perform other tasks similar to Georghiades' (2000) metacognitive instances. In addition to giving students a tool for learning, interactive notebooks allow teachers to probe student understanding and to provide supportive feedback; they also turn into a portfolio of sorts to assist in assessing student progress and can act as a conduit for teacher feedback. We have heard that parents like interactive notebooks, too; for many of them, this is the first time that they have been able to really "see" how their students are thinking in school.

So, Why Joyful Learning?

"That was a fun class, but I learned a lot, too." We began this chapter by noting that students often think of fun and learning as mutually exclusive. Attention to motivation and engagement—the starting point for joyful learning—is critical for sustained learning in mathematics and science. In *Engaging Minds in the Classroom*, Opitz and Ford (2014) distilled why the joyful learning framework is so effective in helping students succeed and become lifelong learners:

It capitalizes on what we know about how to best motivate students. Schweinle and colleagues (2006) stated that "optimal levels of challenge, coupled with affective and motivational support, can provide contexts more supportive of students' feelings of enjoyment, efficacy, and value in mathematics" (p. 289). Understanding the varied factors that affect motivation helps us as teachers to intentionally design classroom cultures where students feel they can be successful. We can design experiences for students driven by their interests—which will increase the value that they place on learning—and we can design tasks that hit the "sweet spot" of providing challenge that motivates instead of terrifying (or boring) our students.

It enables us to build on what we currently know about engagement. When learners are engaged, they voluntarily commit to the learning task and persist through challenging situations. They find value in what they are learning and seek to understand, not just to perform. By understanding motivation and its relationship to engagement, we can move beyond fun activities with fleeting learning toward purposeful and meaningful activities with deep learning in mathematics and science.

It enables us to focus on the whole child. The "whole child" embraces many attributes, including being intellectually active; creative and curious; empathetic; kind, caring, and fair; and able to think critically (ASCD, 2007). The joyful learning framework focuses on both the cognitive and the affective aspects of learning. Joyful learning nurtures emotional well-being, intellectual engagement, and prosocial behaviors.

It acknowledges that the learner is influenced by the contexts in which learning takes place. The learning process and knowledge construction is the result of individuals interacting in social environments to make sense of experiences. Therefore, it is impossible to separate what is being learned from the culture within which it is being learned. The disconnect between students' identity—their perception of themselves as a whole, including their perception of themselves as learners—and the way that they perceive mathematics and science as a discipline is often striking. This disconnect is more profound with students from backgrounds that are traditionally underrepresented in math and science (Burke & Stets, 2009). If students do not find joy in learning math and science, how will they ever be able to imagine themselves as scientists or mathematicians?

Conclusion

Joyful teaching and learning moments may seem magical; our goal is to empower you to create those magical moments during your science and mathematics teaching. In this chapter, we peeked behind the curtain of these magical moments to identify the affective factors that lead to joyful learning. In order to make best use of this new understanding, however, you must evaluate the education environment in which your students learn. In the next chapter, we discuss how to assess how well five elements of your environmental setting contribute to joyful learning.

CHAPTER 2

Evaluating and Assessing
Joyful Learning

Learners, teachers, texts and materials, assessments, and schoolwide configurations largely determine the methods that teachers use in their practice and influence their attitudes toward teaching. These five elements also can dictate the methods that students put into practice and shape their attitudes toward learning. In this chapter, we examine how evaluating our students, ourselves as teachers, the texts and materials we use, our math and science assessments, and schoolwide configurations is essential to setting the stage for joyful learning in science and mathematics.

Evaluating Learners

In evaluating learners in science and mathematics (see Figure 2.1), we are guided by the essential questions that Opitz and Ford identified in *Engaging Minds in the Classroom* (2014):

- Do learners think they can succeed?
- Do learners want to succeed?
- Do learners know what they need to do to succeed?

If students believe they can succeed, if they want to succeed, and if they know how to succeed, they will find joyful learning—and their teachers will experience joyful teaching—in science and mathematics.

FIGURE 2.1

Evaluating Learners in Science and Mathematics

Identity	How do my students identify with science? How do my students identify with mathematics?
Self-efficacy	Do my students believe they can be successful at mastering science? Do my students believe they can be successful at mastering mathematics?
Curiosity and interest	Do my students exhibit curiosity about math and science? Do my students show interest in math and science? Do my students seek out math and science topics (e.g., nonfiction "free reading") when given a choice?
Value	Do my students place importance on understanding math and science? Do my students see connections between math and science and their lives? Do my students think learning math and science is worth the cost (investment of their time and energy)?
Perception of challenge	How do my students evince their perceptions of their skill? How do students perceive the task's challenge?
Goal orientation	Do my students seek to understand (mastery goal) or to perform (performance goal)? How do my students react to failure?
Self-regulating behaviors	Do my students self-evaluate and reflect on their own learning? Are they able to explain their thinking and problem-solving processes?
Persistence	Do my students persevere when faced with a challenging learning task?
Prosocial behaviors	To what extent do my students participate in our community of learners?

Identity and self-efficacy affect whether learners *think* they can succeed. Students' personal beliefs (*self-efficacy*) include their perceived abilities to learn science and mathematics. Bandura (1986) noted that "among different aspects of self-knowledge, perhaps none is as influential in people's everyday lives than conceptions of their personal efficacy" (p. 390). Students with low self-efficacy in science and mathematics tend to perceive problems as too challenging, even before attempting them—and this can lead to math anxiety and learned helplessness.

The overarching question is, do *all* of our students feel capable of learning science, technology, engineering, and math (STEM) content? Recent studies have suggested that students of color do not participate in science classes due to their ethnic and gender identity (Gilbert & Yerrick, 2001; Nasir & Saxe, 2003); ELLs face challenges learning scientific and mathematical language (Lee & Fradd, 1998). Learner identity is loosely shaped by personal beliefs, conceptions about science and mathematics, the teacher, and the context of the classroom and school. Identity is dynamic, however, and can change over time. Teachers have a great deal of power to encourage a positive construction of learner identity in the science and mathematics classroom.

During her years teaching, Michelle found that several of her students staunchly believed that they did not look or act like scientists or mathematicians. By 4th grade, many of her students were convinced that learning math and science, or having a career in science and mathematics, was unattainable—and, unfortunately, these beliefs had been engendered by other adults in their lives (e.g., parents, grandparents, caregivers, former teachers). Several other students deliberately did not complete labs and activities or fully share their ideas in fear of appearing "smart" in front of their peers. Michelle wanted her students to perceive science and mathematics as ways of knowing and ways of solving problems, rather than memorizing and retaining factual information. She made an effort to debunk students' misconceptions by introducing them to professionals in the field, providing them opportunities to research and read about professionals and their work, and educating students about the vast vocational prospects that use scientific and mathematical knowledge.

> ELL students' identity, efficacy, and anxiety can be affected by their perceived abilities in conversational English, math and science content knowledge, and the language proficiency required by the content.

As we discussed in Chapter 1, curiosity, interest, value, and perception of challenge all affect student motivation and engagement. What are your students curious about? What are their interests? What do they value? How do your students perceive challenging tasks in the classroom? Students' interests, values, and perceptions can mimic those of their teachers. Teaching elementary school science content only on Friday afternoons or hurriedly at the end of the academic year compels students to question its value. A high school biology teacher who relies solely on textbook reading and rote memorization, and does not engage students in conversations or hands-on activities to promote deeper understanding, sends the message that the content itself is a chore and tedious.

Problem solving should be an engaging activity for students and teachers, rather than a chore and bore. There are many ways to nurture motivated and complex thinkers, readers, and writers. Illustrating for students the "aha!" moments of inspiration and understanding sends the message that the content—including the challenges it may present—is exciting and worth exploring. An inquiry-based approach, where students' questions guide their exploration, has been shown to enhance content knowledge and comprehension (Marshall, 2013, Romance & Vitale, 2005). Ketelhut (2007) investigated whether changing the environment might improve middle school students' self-efficacy on scientific inquiry skills. She found that a multi-user virtual environment (i.e., computer-game-based) improved students' self-efficacy and learning processes. Teachers who assist and guide students to challenge themselves and their thinking tend to increase positive student self-efficacy regarding science and mathematics.

> Settings that facilitate student-guided inquiry have been shown to enhance progress in ELLs' second-language learning and increase the frequency of their contributions to content-related discussions and strategy use (Krashen, 1987; Varelas & Pappas, 2006).

Goal orientation, self-regulating behaviors, persistence, and prosocial behaviors influence learners if learners *know* what they need to do to succeed. Students (and teachers) need time: time to think and reflect and rethink and reflect, again and again; time to communicate in various ways (e.g., drawing, writing, speaking); and time to develop and practice social skills (i.e., listening, presenting, promoting and encouraging peers, resolving conflicts and arguing).

Evaluating Ourselves as Teachers

Teachers are the key influential factor in student achievement (Haycock, 1998; Lynch, 2000). If we do not believe that we can teach science and mathematics, then we are probably not teaching science and mathematics effectively. Clark and Groves (2012) asserted that teachers who are emotionally invested in student learning and who perceive themselves as "scientific thinkers" understand why science content is relevant for their students and are more capable of knowing how to teach science. We decide, every day, whether we are going to turn students on or off to science and mathematics in our classrooms. Eric distinctly remembers times as a teacher when he was able to excite students about learning science by incorporating current events or demonstrating explicit connections between concepts and the real world. He also learned the hard way that a mismatch between perceived challenge and student ability and cutting off "sense making" during a whole-class discussion were quick ways to turn students off to learning.

Researchers suggest a strong connection between teachers' epistemology and instructional practices, particularly when the teacher attempts to create a constructivist learning environment (reviewed in Jones & Carter, 2007; Kane, Sandretto, & Heath, 2002; Pajares, 1996). Teachers must continually assess their understanding and consider their own perceptions of the nature of science and mathematics, and confront their naïve or negative views. Midgley, Feldlaufer, and Eccles (1989) found that middle school students' self-efficacy regarding mathematics and mathematical problem solving reflected their teachers' self-efficacy. Jones and Carter's (2007) sociocultural model of embedded belief systems postulated that teachers' beliefs and attitudes affect their concept of knowledge and content acquisition—and, hence, the way they present material. Our prior experiences influence our beliefs, as well as how we perceive new experiences. This is why changing beliefs is so complex: Not only do we need to be explicit with our students when we teach science and mathematics, and confront their views and beliefs, but we also need to be open and honest with ourselves. We need to recognize our own identity and self-efficacy. In assessing ourselves as teachers (see Figure 2.2), we must investigate and reflect on the instructional methods as well as the attitudes and perceptions—and passion—we transfer to our students.

Jarvis and Lewis (2002) noted that many schools emphasize problem solving over "the more creative endeavor of problem finding" (p.129). Problem finding—the combination of common sense, reasoning, and divergent

FIGURE 2.2

Assessing Ourselves as Teachers

Identity	How do I identify with science?	How do I help my students better identify with math and science?
	How do I identify with mathematics?	
Self-efficacy	Am I confident that I can be successful in teaching science?	How can I improve my students' confidence in their ability to be successful at mastering science and math?
	Am I confident that I can be successful in teaching mathematics?	
	Do I get frustrated and anxious when encountering a challenging math problem, or when trying to decide how best to present a science concept?	How do I help my students minimize anxiety?
Curiosity and interest	Am I curious about mathematics and science topics?	How do I foster my students' curiosity and personal interests in math and science?
	Do I demonstrate my interest in mathematics and science?	How do I seek to generate situational interest for my students in mathematics and science tasks?
	Do I seek opportunities to learn more about science and mathematics (e.g., attend lectures or presentations, read science or math news)?	
Value	Do I place importance on my understanding of math and science?	How do I help my students understand the importance of understanding math and science, and the application of content to their lives?
	Do I try to identify connections between math and science in my life, and point them out to my students?	
Perception of challenge	Do I proactively monitor student perceptions of their own skill and their perceptions of task challenge?	How do I help learners know what they need to do to succeed?
Goal orientation	Do I exhibit teaching behaviors that promote a mastery-goal orientation?	How do I help students understand that mistakes and failure are a natural part of the learning process?
Self-regulating behaviors	Do I model self-regulating behaviors?	How do I help my students effectively reflect on their learning and apply this to their future learning?
Persistence	Do I model perseverance when faced with a challenging learning task?	How do I help my students persevere when faced with a challenging learning task?
Prosocial behavior	Have I created a classroom community of learners that values prosocial behaviors?	How do I help my students participate in our classroom community of learners?

thinking that leads to deeper exploration of content—is essential to the process of joyful learning. Are these traits we demonstrate to our students, as teachers of science and mathematics?

Evaluating Texts and Materials

Attitudes and perceptions about curriculum and pedagogy strongly influence the way educators teach (Cobern & Loving, 2002). Time is precious in our classrooms, and it seems that "playing" with materials or manipulatives, learning by doing, and attending to self-reflection are often subtracted from the curriculum. For the reasons of time and the joy of learning, it is essential to evaluate the texts and materials we use in our classrooms, to ensure that all components work together to help our students grasp the relevance of the content and how it is connected to content within the disciplines of science and mathematics, as well as to help them identify connections with other disciplines.

Rosser (1995) suggested that students are more attracted to scientific methods when they see a connection with other disciplines and the usefulness of content knowledge. This is particularly true for girls and for students of color (O'Brien, Martinez-Pons, & Kopala, 1999; Rosebery, Warren, & Conant, 1992), who have traditionally encountered barriers to accessing science material (i.e., masculine perspective) and to pursuing science careers (Rosser, 1995). The result is a group of students who are often disengaged in high school science classes (Schmidt, Smith, & Shumow, 2009) and decreasingly participate in mathematics and science (Gilbert & Yerrick, 2001).

To offset disengagement, as teachers we need to explore new ways of connecting students and content. Michelle worked on a study of 1st graders' conceptions of linear measurement (Clarkson, Robelia, Chahine, Fleming, & Lawrenz, 2007), which included girls and students of color. The lesson built on real classroom experiences and allowed students to work through a series of problems using various lined rulers. Students identified patterns between the different rulers they used and were excited about measuring. Michelle still recalls one girl's excitement about using her new knowledge to help her grandmother redesign their kitchen. As a teacher, Michelle helped design a crime scene investigation (CSI) lesson plan for a 6th grade team whose students included ELLs. Students investigated the scene, interviewed potential suspects, and recorded conclusions based on evidence they discovered. Michelle had never seen so many students writing and motivated to learn more about CSI methods and scientific content. Not only was every student in every classroom motivated to write, but students also learned to communicate scientific content in a variety of ways (i.e., newspaper writing, recording and documenting evidence, legal court case reporting, delivering mock trials).

To ensure that ELLs have access to the same level of content as other students in the class (and hence can engage with both the content and classroom discussion and activities), teachers may need to differentiate text and materials based on language proficiency stage.

Therefore, when assessing the texts and materials we use in science and math classrooms, we must evaluate whether everything we use is accessible to all of our students and supports their identities as learners:

- Do students see people like themselves reflected in the texts and materials we use?
- Do texts and materials provide student with tools, hints, or suggestions that assist them in problem solving?
- Are there sufficient quantities of texts and materials to provide students with choice and autonomy in different activities?
- Do texts and materials help students see the connection between math and science and their lives?
- Do texts and materials provide differentiated levels of task challenge?
- Are texts and materials designed to encourage student self-reflection?

Assessments in Science and Mathematics

When students struggle to pass a test, teachers often employ more guided instructional methods and teach to the assessment. However, a better response might be to rethink how we use assessments. A focus on formative assessment, what Stiggins (2005) calls "assessments for learning," can increase students' self-efficacy, promote mastery-goal orientation, and improve student learning. Formative assessment should be narrowly focused on specific learning outcomes, easy for students to complete, and used frequently (at least twice per week). The most effective formative assessment, however, fits naturally within the flow of a lesson. Analyze, but don't grade, formative assessment; this is simply a status check

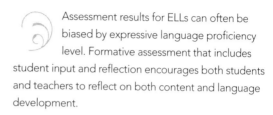

Assessment results for ELLs can often be biased by expressive language proficiency level. Formative assessment that includes student input and reflection encourages both students and teachers to reflect on both content and language development.

on student progress toward your learning goals. Analyzing your results should lead to instructional decisions for whole-group and individualized instruction.

Remember that students need individual feedback, and they need it as soon as possible. After reviewing nearly 8,000 studies on instruction and learning, John Hattie (2009) concluded that providing systematic feedback in relation to learning objectives is the single most powerful innovation for improving student achievement. Feedback that emphasizes an overall judgment or a grade, however, can hamper the learning process due to "ego involvement" (Black & Harrison, 2004), and students respond with a performance orientation ("How did I do in relation to others?"). In contrast, feedback that emphasizes strengths and weaknesses of student work and suggests next steps in the learning process improves learning and engagement through *task involvement*. This helps students develop mastery goals ("What could I do differently?"). Self-reflection is also essential and helps students "[watch] themselves grow, [feel] in control of their success, and [believe] that continued success is within reach if they keep trying" (Stiggins, 2005, p. 328).

In his classes, Eric uses exit and entrance tickets, quick writes, and "muddiest points" prompts to probe students' understanding of concepts. These simple strategies are great for collecting data to make instructional decisions. He also uses a few different strategies for helping students to reflect on their understanding. One is to make a simple list of concepts and then phrase them as "I can" statements (e.g., "I can explain the difference between velocity and acceleration"). Another strategy is to provide students with a worksheet that includes learning objectives; students fill in what they know at the beginning, in the middle, and near the end of a unit. Each time they write, students use a different ink color and include specific experiences that helped add to their understanding of the concept. This approach is a great way for students to explicitly link the work they are doing for class to the concepts that they are learning.

The assessments we use in science and mathematics classrooms should

• Support students' identification of themselves as mathematics and science learners.

• Measure a wide range of beliefs and attitudes toward science and mathematics, as well as assess students' demonstration of content acquisition.

• Include different formats (e.g., individual, small-group assessment).

• Require students to make connections and reflect on their learning of the content.

• Ask students to share the usefulness of the teaching/learning experience.

• Offer complex problem-solving opportunities.

Evaluating Schoolwide Configurations

Joyful learning of science and mathematics needs to be supported and encouraged within the school context. At the elementary level, reading, writing, and mathematics traditionally have been emphasized; science's rightful place in the curriculum continues to be debated (Appleton, 2007). At this level, science often is integrated into the other core subject areas as an add-on rather than presented as an integral part of the curriculum. In addition, schools struggle to meet local, state, and national expectations. Teachers in middle and high school face challenges such as identifying engaging additional resources to support student understanding and engagement with the content—while preparing students for high-stakes tests.

Science and mathematics should enjoy a schoolwide focus throughout the academic year. When we develop and implement family STEM events or gradually build and sustain resources and materials that support all teachers in the school (at the elementary level) or that science and math teachers can share and compare (at middle and high school), we are emphasizing the connection to students' lives and promoting the idea that these content areas are exciting and accessible to all. Starting this process in elementary school—

particularly in schools and classrooms with students from underrepresented groups—lays the foundation for continued growth in students' perception of themselves as learners in these subjects.

To understand how schoolwide configurations relate to joy of learning in science and math classrooms, consider how schoolwide configurations influence your decisions about teaching science and mathematics and the beliefs your colleagues and administrators have toward these subjects. How do these perceptions affect teachers, students, and the school community? Is there support for promoting science and mathematics educational efforts? Does the school community share interests and new knowledge from the field? Does the school climate encourage students in mastery or performance goal orientation? Are there opportunities for greater participation in and access to science and math activities? And, most important, do teachers encourage school leaders to support science and mathematics education?

Moving Forward in Science and Mathematics

To move forward in science and mathematics education, we have to continually question and reflect on our students, ourselves, our texts and materials, our assessments, and the schoolwide configurations that influence our decision-making process. Identity is dynamic and can change over time, giving us an opportunity as teachers to cultivate and sustain positive identities in our students.

Students need to identify with science and mathematics and be able to see the relevance of the content beyond the classroom walls. They need to think of themselves as capable learners of science and mathematics, and we need to approach all students as capable learners of science and mathematics. As teachers, we need to be explicit about the choices we make in terms of activities, texts, materials, and assessments. We need to keep in mind our students' identities as learners of science and mathematics. We need to promote positive student identity, improve student self-efficacy, and increase student interest in and value of the content in order to encourage students in science and mathematics.

How can you pursue these goals in your own school and classroom? In the next chapter, we discuss specific strategies for promoting joyful learning in science and math classrooms. We identify how to promote joyful learning in five key areas and provide examples of activities that will enhance students' identities as science and math learners.

CHAPTER 3

Implementing Joyful Learning in Science and Math

In the book *Pinkalicious: School Rules!* (Kann, 2010), Pinkalicious is sad because she cannot bring her best friend, an imaginary unicorn, to school with her. At first, her teacher says that it is against the rules for unicorns to be in school. A little later in the book, the unicorn comes to school with her and causes some mischief. Eventually, the teacher relents and Pinkalicious, her unicorn, and her friends have a wonderful time playing together. At first glance, it may not seem as though Pinkalicious has much to do with joyful learning. However, the book is a great illustration of the creative energies of young children and the dangers of ignoring that creativity at school. Pinkalicious was sad and bored and started getting into trouble—until her teacher freed her to be creative.

Something similar happens when math and science students are given the opportunity to be creative. Challenging students to develop a project of their choosing, or to apply what they know in a hands-on activity or to their "real" life, unleashes student creativity with fantastic results and can provide the opportunity for mentoring and feedback. Incorporating creativity, choice, and autonomy helps build students' self-efficacy, keeps them motivated, and strengthens their identities as scientists and mathematicians.

Strategies for Joyful Learning

In *Engaging Minds in the Classroom* (2014), Opitz and Ford presented a framework to help teachers purposefully select strategies and activities that promote joyful learning. The framework is rooted in research about motivation (see Chapter 1) and is applied in five key areas: school community, the physical environment (i.e., the classroom), whole-group instruction, small-group instruction, and individual instruction. Different activity structures can then be used within the framework to emphasize aspects of joyful learning. In this chapter, we identify structures and provide examples of activities (see Figure 3.1) that

- Build on students' personal interest or generate situational interest;
- Help students focus on understanding concepts (mastery-goal orientation) rather than simply earning a grade (performance orientation);

FIGURE 3.1
Implementing the Joyful Learning Framework in Science and Mathematics

Learning environment/configuration	Rationale	Structure	Sample activity
School community	Create a positive schoolwide climate that promotes learning in math and science	Schoolwide events	Math Methods Madness Day
			Science Books & Films Prize mock election
Classroom environment	Reinforce students' perceptions of themselves as scientists and mathematicians	Identity builders	Identity posters
			Citizen Science
Whole-group instruction	Engage all learners	Active participation and thinking	What Questions Do You Have?
			It's a (Math) Date!
Small-group instruction	Promote social interaction	Vocabulary development	Connections flashcards
		Technology integration	Show Me the Concept
		Assessment	Multicolor quiz
Individual instruction	Allow choice and incorporate students' interests	Choice	Choice challenges
		Unleashing creativity	Cosmic Comic

- Allow for differentiation of task challenge;
- Encourage students to identify themselves as scientists and mathematicians; and
- Provide opportunities for teacher feedback and student self-reflection.

School Community

Our classrooms exist within a larger school community; the values and norms of a school often set the tone for individual classrooms. A positive school climate sets the table for joyful learning to occur within and across classrooms. The opposite is true, too: a negative school climate presents an obstacle to overcome when aiming for joyful learning in mathematics and science. A successful schoolwide joyful learning environment capitalizes on student interests, stresses content mastery over (implicit or explicit) student comparisons, and supports affective outcomes. In the best cases, this type of supportive learning community is visible the minute you enter the building: celebrations of student work line the hallways, pictures and posters provide a peek into the exciting things that students are doing, and artifacts are on display highlighting students' athletic prowess, musical ability, and theatrical skills. However, how often do you see examples of student work in STEM fields?

The Structure: Schoolwide Events

If we want students to find joy in learning math and science, we should celebrate their work. If we want to encourage them to see themselves as scientists and mathematicians, and to consider pursuing STEM studies, we need to showcase students' work in these disciplines alongside their work in other areas. One way to do this is to hold schoolwide events designed specifically to celebrate mathematics and science. Considerations when designing an event include the following:

- Does the activity allow students to creatively approach and demonstrate their mastery of the math and science curriculum?
- Does the event appeal equally to boys and girls, and celebrate the skills of diverse learners?
- Does the activity require students to apply knowledge aligned with grade-level math and science standards?

• Does it engage students to work collaboratively and recognize and celebrate one another's accomplishments?

Designing a schoolwide event that meets these criteria not only enables students to demonstrate content mastery, but also appeals to their creativity and interests, increases motivation and engagement, and enhances their sense of belonging to a community of learners.

The Activity: Math Methods Madness Day

Reform efforts in mathematics over the last two decades have placed a much greater emphasis on student understanding of mathematical concepts. Instead of mathematical algorithms, students use intuitive strategies to solve problems. Inventing strategies or correctly using multiple strategies to solve the same type of problem helps students conceptualize the mathematics principles at work.

On Math Methods Madness Day, students solve developmentally appropriate story problems in small collaborative groups. Instead of just seeking the right answer, students are challenged to find as many different ways to represent and solve the problem as they can. Students then create posters, slideshows, or videos (depending on grade level) to illustrate the different successful and unsuccessful strategies they explored. Projects should include student annotation or narration that addresses whether and why each strategy worked, which supports student learning: "Monitoring and reflecting during problem solving helps students think about what they are doing and why they are doing it, evaluate the steps they are taking to solve the problem, and connect new concepts to what they already know" (What Works Clearinghouse, 2012, p. 17). After students complete their projects, a gallery walk allows them to see how their classmates approached and solved the same problem. As noted in the WWC report, "When students see the various methods employed by others, they learn to approach and solve

Modeling and teaching students to use multiple strategies, in addition to supporting students' ability to conceptualize principles, provides ELLs with repeated exposure to new and necessary academic vocabulary.

problems in different ways" (p. 36). Having a follow-up class discussion will reinforce this aspect of problem solving as well as support students in identifying the approaches or strategies they felt worked best for them—which they can use in solving problems in the future. Figure 3.2 illustrates two students' different approaches to solving the same fractions problem, as well as their explanations of their strategies.

Math Methods Madness Day can be done as a classroom event, but why not hold it schoolwide? The gallery walk could be an evening event for families, giving them a chance to see student work in the classroom setting. At the middle or high school level, a competition could identify the most creative, time-saving, or unusual problem-solving approaches. The Inside Mathematics website's problems of the month series is perfect for a Math Methods Madness event. Each problem of the month provides a set of leveled problems, ranging from early elementary through high school, focused on the same context. See www.insidemathematics.org/index.php/tools-for-teachers/problems-of-the-month.

Combining the Math Methods Madness Day with another school spirit event (e.g., crazy hair day or student assembly), scheduling it for the end of a semester or grading period, and holding a schoolwide celebration has the potential for making the event into something students anticipate and in which they willingly participate. To strengthen the relationship between different age groups, older students could create problems for younger students to solve, or students from different grade levels could work together. A schoolwide follow-up activity might include having students or classes nominate problems for the next scheduled Math Methods Madness Day.

Math Methods Madness Day can easily be translated as a Science Solutions Day, with students solving real-life science challenges. The Discovery Education/3M Young Scientist Challenge website (http://www.youngscientist challenge.com/) provides resources and links for student projects and classroom activities.

The Activity: Mock Election for Science Books and Films Prize

Students have many opportunities in school to read fiction, but not nearly as many opportunities to read high-quality nonfiction (Dreher & Voelker,

FIGURE 3.2

Examples of Student Problem Solving with Reflection

Problem[115]

Find the area of this pentagon.

Solution strategies

Ali and Maria each worked on this problem individually. After 20 minutes in a small-group activity, they talked to each other about how they approached the problem.

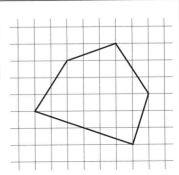

ALI: The pentagon is slanted, so first I looked for figures for which I knew how to compute the area. Look what I found: Six right triangles inside; and they get rid of the slanted parts, so what's left are rectangles.

Then, I noticed that the right triangles are really three pairs of congruent right triangles. So together, the ones marked 1 have an area of 2 x 3 = 6 square units. The ones marked 2 combine for an area of 3 x 1 = 3 square units. The ones marked 3 also combine for an area of 3 square units.

What's left inside is a 2-by-3 rectangle, with an area of 6 square units; a 1-by-4 rectangle, with an area of 4 square units; and a 1-by-3 rectangle, with an area of 3 square units.

So the area of the pentagon is 6 + 3 +3 + 6 + 4 + 3 = 25 square units.

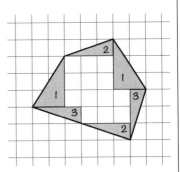

MARIA: You looked inside the pentagon, but I looked outside to deal with the slanted parts. I saw that I could put the pentagon inside a rectangle. I colored in the pentagon and figured if I could subtract the area of the white space from the area of the rectangle, I'd have the area of the pentagon.

I know the area of the rectangle is 6 x 7 = 42 square units.

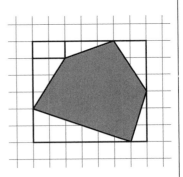

I saw that the white space was really five right triangles plus a little rectangle. The little rectangle is 1-by-2 units, so its area is 1 x 2 = 2 square units. Then, I figured the areas of the five right triangles: 1.5 square units, 1.5 square units, 3 square units, 3 square units, and 6 square units. So the area of the white space is 2 + 1.5 + 1.5 + 3 + 3 + 6 = 17 square units.

To get the area of the pentagon, I subtracted 17 from 42 and, like you, I got 25 square units for the area of the pentagon.

Source: Reprinted from *What Works Clearinghouse,* 2012, p. 36.

2004). With few exceptions, science trade books geared toward elementary, middle, and high school students are written by adults, reviewed by adults, and given awards by adults—with little input from the children who are expected to read them. The purpose of the Science Books and Films Prize mock election is to engage students in reading, reviewing, and discussing the merits of high-quality science trade books.

Science Books and Films (SB&F) is a free monthly online publication of the American Association for the Advancement of Science that focuses on science resources from a variety of media, for all ages. In late fall, the publication lists finalists in various categories (e.g., picture books, hands-on science activities, video and software), and a panel of librarians, scientists, and science literacy experts identifies the best in each. Gerber, Hartman, and Brunsell (2009) used the idea of the awards to develop a mock election project for students, which has been successfully implemented in a variety of grade levels.

As a classroom activity, all students read the same teacher-selected books and complete a judging form or rubric to facilitate discussion. Another resource for grade-level-appropriate texts is the National Science Teachers Association/Children's Book Council outstanding science trade books list.

The rubric should prompt students to assess how well the books present scientific concepts and how well they are written, as well as the books' appeal to their age group and to a wide range of students. Small groups of students discuss

 Small-group work and discussion reduces ELLs' anxiety and increases their opportunities to participate more often than in whole-class instruction (Echevarria, Vogt, & Short, 2012).

the merits of each book. For the award portion of the activity, each group nominates a book for the best award and then presents a case for its selection, or the class decides via whole-class discussion and vote.

As a schoolwide activity, groups of students or classes from each grade level prepare posters, slideshow presentations, or videos. Displaying posters or showing videos and slide presentations during all-school announcements will also support the identification of students as part of a community of learners.

As with the classroom structure, an all-school awards ceremony or assembly culminates the activity, perhaps including participation of the authors of the nominated books (either in person or via distance technology (e.g., Skype); students can submit questions in advance for authors to address. The Science Books and Film website (http://www.sbfonline.com/) also has a collection of video book talks that include authors discussing winning publications. The book talks could be incorporated into the schoolwide activity. In addition, this idea can be recast as a Best Science Resources competition, with students and classrooms nominating their favorite science websites and Internet resources.

Classroom Environment

The classroom environment strongly influences how students identify themselves as learners. Issues surrounding identity are particularly important for science and mathematics; student persistence in STEM content areas throughout their elementary and secondary years (and beyond) is closely related to their perceptions of these subjects (Brickhouse, Lowery, & Schultz, 2000; Hill, Corbett, & St. Rose, 2010). Often, students perceive scientists and mathematicians as older white men, and the subjects as disciplines that are rigid, uncreative, and individualistic (Carlone & Johnson, 2007; Olitsky, 2006). By creating a classroom environment that values science and mathematics, teachers can portray a more authentic view of the disciplines and help students envision themselves in the world of science and math.

To expand ELLs' view of potential professions in science and math, include historic representations from different cultural and linguistic backgrounds.

The Structure: Identity Builders

Opitz and Ford (2014) described identity builders as a structure that can help students view themselves as successful learners, because the structure requires students to "actively interact with their learning and make links between what they learn and themselves, their knowledge, and their own experiences" (p. 51). Students' perceptions of themselves often conflict with their views of what it takes to be "good at" science and mathematics. This conflict begins in elementary school, but it becomes even more pronounced in middle school as adolescents try to determine their place within that setting; as observed in the book and film *Diary of a Wimpy Kid*, "you can't recover from social suicide." For girls, there is often the added pressure of math and science being perceived as unsuitable content areas. Danica McKellar (a child actress who later pursued a doctorate in mathematics) has been widely quoted as saying "There is an epidemic right now of girls dumbing themselves down . . . in middle school because they think it makes them attractive." Incorporating identity-building activities in the classroom environment can help students identify the real-life application of math and science concepts, as well as promote a more authentic view of their consideration of their own future roles in STEM fields.

The Activity: Identity Posters

Most science and math classrooms have posters on the walls illustrating concepts and problem-solving approaches, or describing famous professionals in the field. These posters are nice, but they have one tragic flaw: they are created by adults. Having students interact with their science and math environment reinforces their perception of themselves as learners in these content areas—and this is the goal of the identity posters activity.

This activity can be as simple as hanging a piece of chart paper on the wall with the phrase "Mathematicians Are Creative" in the center. Then, throughout the year, students add examples as they encounter creative uses of mathematics in books, movies, and real-life experiences—with sticky notes, photos, or other decoration. Students also can use the class poster to capture examples of themselves being creative as they solve challenging mathematics problems. This ongoing activity could culminate with students using the interactive poster to create a project illustrating why mathematics is a creative endeavor (e.g., written essay, slideshow, or video).

For students in middle and high school, this idea can be extended to having students create posters profiling a professional in a STEM field; students could either profile a historical figure that describes the individual's contribution or interview and profile a local professional. Another identity-poster approach for this population would be to have students research careers in the field and create a poster or advertisement describing the job, education requirements, and typical skills required. The U.S. Department of Labor website (http://www.onetonline.org/) is user friendly and has extensive career resources; this assignment has the added benefit of helping students actively investigate potential careers and plan for them.

The Activity: Citizen Science

Students often have a disconnect between what they view as "school science" and "real science." Incorporating citizen science projects gives students an authentic view of what scientists do and broadens the learning environment beyond the four walls of the classroom. Loree Griffin Burns's *Citizen Scientists: Be a Part of Scientific Discovery From Your Own Backyard* (2012) describes *citizen science* as

> the study of our world by the people who live in it. Not just professional people—scientists with degrees and laboratories and fancy equipment—but everyday people, too. All men, women, and children who use their senses and smarts to understand the world around them can be citizen scientists. (p. 5)

Citizen science projects are developed by scientists so that they can conduct much larger investigations than would be possible if they tried to do it alone. Many of these projects are suitable for elementary and secondary school classrooms, including

• The Cornell Lab of Ornithology (http://www.birds.cornell.edu/citsci /projects): Seven citizen science projects focusing on the habitats and species of birds. Data from students' work are used by scientists in a variety of ways to map habitat locations around the world.

• NOVA Labs' Sun Lab (http://www.pbs.org/wgbh/nova/labs/lab/sun/): Video collection focusing on solar storms, with an ongoing "open investigation" to support work in predicting solar activity.

• NASA's Students' Cloud Observations Online (http://scool.larc.nasa .gov/): Classroom-designed projects for students to observe and report on cloud changes and compare these to satellite views.

• The FoldIt Online Protein Puzzle (http://fold.it/portal/info/science): Online game playing results contribute to research on the structure of proteins, with the goal of assisting in identifying treatment for chronic diseases and creating new fuel sources.

- Zooniverse (https://www.zooniverse.org/), Scientific American (http://www.scientificamerican.com/citizen-science/), and SciStarter.org (http://www.scistarter.com/) provide access to dozens of additional citizen science projects for all grade levels.

Whole-Group Instruction

During whole-group instruction, it can be easy for individual students to become anonymous and disengaged. In this key area, it is essential to focus on the *context* of learning as well as the learners themselves. For joyful learning to occur in whole-group instruction, students need to be engaged in meaningful and interesting activities or discussions with appropriate challenge.

The Structure: Active Participation and Thinking

To engage students in whole-group instruction, incorporate activities that require students to think like scientists or mathematicians. The Common Core State Standards for Mathematics (CCSS; National Governors Association Center for Best Practices, Council of Chief State School Officers, 2010, pp. 6–8) and the Next Generation Science Standards (NGSS; Achieve, Inc., 2013, Appendix F) each include eight practices that define essential skills and thought processes (see Figure 3.3).

The Activity: What Questions Do You Have?

STEM professionals are driven to explain the world around them. They ask questions, collect evidence, and use that evidence to construct explanations and arguments. Helping students develop skills related to questioning is engaging and well suited to whole-group instruction. After winning a Nobel Prize for physics, Isidor Isaac Rabi reflected on how his mother, rather than asking if he learned anything in school, would ask if he had asked any good questions. He noted, "That difference—asking good questions—made me become a good scientist" (Sackler, n.d.). Helping students learn to ask good questions is a three-step process that can be practiced during whole-group instruction.

FIGURE 3.3	
Active Participation and Thinking in Math and Science	
CCSS Mathematics	**Next Generation Science Standards**
• Make sense of problems and persevere in solving them.	• Ask questions and define problems.
• Model with mathematics.	• Develop and use models.
• Construct viable arguments and critique the reasoning of others.	• Engage in argument from evidence. • Construct explanations and design solutions.
• Use appropriate tools strategically.	• Plan and carry out investigations.
• Reason abstractly and quantitatively. Attend to precision.	• Use mathematics and computational thinking.
• Look for and make use of structure. • Look for and express regularity in repeated reasoning.	• Analyze and interpret data.
	• Obtain, evaluate, and communicate information.

1. *Understand the context.* Our colleagues Tim and Stephanie Slater are fond of saying, "It is impossible to ask questions in a vacuum." Students need something to ask questions about; provide context by using realia, images, audio, or video related to the topic being studied. For example, Eric often uses a time-lapse video of a rotting bowl of fruit as questioning context for a unit on plant life cycles.

2. *Brainstorm questions.* The key to brainstorming activities is to encourage students to be nonjudgmental; rather than worrying about asking good or bad questions, they should feel free to ask as many questions as possible. As a part of whole-group instruction, have students brainstorm by writing their questions on a chalkboard, interactive whiteboard, sentence strips taped to a wall, or chart paper. Brainstorming publicly is more likely to engage all students because other students' ideas spark additional questions, generate interest, and foster excitement.

3. *Refine the list of questions.* The first time you do this activity, ask students to identify the questions that they find most interesting. Then work with them to identify the characteristics of these interesting questions. Help

students understand that productive questions tend to be open-ended (not a simple yes/no or single-fact response), and practice refining closed questions. As students become more adept at asking questions, you can have them identify and refine questions they can research and those that can lead to hands-on science investigations.

The Activity: It's a (Math) Date!

Many of the CCSS math standards are reinforced when students create, solve, and share their own story problems. Winograd (1992) explained that the process of developing questions deepens students' understanding of how mathematics is related to the world around them.

There are various ways to approach student-created math problems. O'Donnell (2009) described how a 2nd grade teacher had her students explore mathematics by generating as many problems as they could using the date; this basic premise was expanded throughout the school year to incorporate higher-level challenges. Scholastic's Create Your Own Math Hunt (http://www.scholastic.com/teachers/lesson-plan/create-your-own-math-hunt) provides resources appropriate for students through middle school, which can be easily adapted for older students and to provide higher-level challenges. In a Math Hunt activity, students either find or are provided with real-life situations and resources from which to create a story problem. For example, a student given resources related to the human body might learn that the average adult exhales 0.5 liters of air with each breath. Her resulting story problem might read,

> Consider language proficiency when asking students to solve and generate problems. Used correctly, math story problems can be a great way to scaffold academic language development; reinforce with visual representation and supporting evidence.

> Melissa exhales 0.5 liters of air with each breath. On average, she takes 15 breaths per minute. Over the course of a day, how much air does she exhale?

The process of generating questions may be done individually, in pairs, or in small groups; the sharing and solving of these problems, however, is an effective whole-class activity. Having students share their thinking and problem-solving approaches orally, in writing, or with a visual demonstration or representation helps solidify their understanding. It should be noted that sometimes students create questions that involve mathematical concepts they have not yet learned. These can be saved for later in the semester or year, when students are ready to learn the new concept. Using student-created questions when introducing new content to the class enhances their identity as mathematical thinkers and learners as well as their identification with the classroom community.

Small-Group Instruction

Small-group instruction provides an opportune time for students to engage in academic conversations about content. Joyful learning is enhanced in small-group instruction, as students interact socially to explore phenomena and co-construct knowledge.

The Structure: Focused Interaction

The example activities for this key area focus social interactions around expanding vocabulary, using technology to communicate ideas, and deepening understanding through collaborative assessments. These three examples can be used in both math and science classrooms, and they are easily adapted for different grade and ability levels.

The Activity: Connections Flashcards

Mathematics and science are rich with new vocabulary for students to master; this can be challenging because certain terms (e.g., *work, product, theory*) have specific meanings that are different from how they are used in everyday language. Connections flashcards can be used to help students deepen their understanding of vocabulary and how terms are related to each other.

For this activity, small groups of students create flashcards, using either index cards or an online flashcard generator (e.g., Quizlet, http://quizlet.com/; KitzKikz printable, http://www.kitzkikz.com/flashcards/) or app. Vocabulary assigned to each group should come from the same unit and relate to each

FIGURE 3.4

Sample Terms for Connections Flashcards

Grade level	Topic	Vocabulary
Elementary	Math: Number and operations in base 10	less, more, equal, tens digit, ones digit
	Science: Interactions of forces	balanced, unbalanced, forces, motion, magnet, relative size
	Math: Fractions	equivalent, nominator, denominator, decimal, mixed numbers, ratio
Middle/high school	Science: Earth History	sedimentary layers, fossilization, folding, erosion, weathering, water
	Math: Algebra II	associative property, distributive property, commutative property, order of operations, simplification, grouping
	Science: Physics	phase, destructive interference, constructive interference, wavelength, frequency, speed

other, and it may be differentiated for student knowledge and ability levels (see Figure 3.4). In addition to defining the terms, students discuss and settle on connections between the terms. For example, in a geometry unit using the words *angle*, *vertices*, *sides*, *hexagon*, *polygon*, and *square*, students might explain connections by saying, "A polygon has three or more sides. A square is a regular polygon with four sides. A square has four sides of equal length." An additional benefit of this activity is that students can use the flashcards later to review concepts prior to assessment.

The Activity: Show Me the Concept

In this activity, students work in small groups to develop a presentation for their classmates; the process may incorporate technology, enhance social interaction through collaboration, and reinforce student understanding by having students explain a concept or process. Topics should be derived from whole-class instruction or (for high school students) material students are expected to research outside school. For example, 2nd grade students might identify and discuss the difference between even and odd numbers;

middle school science students might introduce basic principles governing heredity and genetics; and high school students might present information on types of chemical bonds.

Ideally, this activity would include allowing student groups to choose among different presentation options (supporting learner autonomy by providing choice):

- An oral presentation, with posters and other visual aids;
- A video lecture (see Lodge McCammon's "paper slides" at http://playingwithmedia.com/2013/03/value-of-low-tech-paper-slide-videos/),
- A slideshow,
- An online presentation (e.g., Prezi, Prezentit); or
- An animated video (using online tools such as GoAnimate 4 Schools).

The Activity: Multicolor Quiz

In Chapters 1 and 2, we discussed the importance of feedback, assessment, and self-reflection to joyful learning in mathematics and science. When feedback is supportive and used to develop understanding, students report higher enjoyment and efficacy (Schweinle, Meyer, & Turner, 2006). Similarly, students who self-reflect on their learning are more engaged, remember more of the lesson, and are more likely to develop mastery-goal orientation. Fluckiger, Vigil, Pasco, and Danielson (2010) found that the multicolor quiz, a simple three-step approach to self-assessment, can lead to decreased anxiety and increased enjoyment:

1. Students take a quiz individually using one color of ink.

2. Students then convene in small groups to discuss the quiz and come to consensus on answers, using a different color of ink.

3. Finally, individually or in small groups, students use their textbook, notes, and other resources to verify answers in a third color of ink.

Individual Instruction

In his article about engaging technologically savvy youth, Prensky (2005) noted that "today's kids are challenging us, their educators, to engage them at their level, even with the old stuff, the stuff we all claim is so important, that is, the 'curriculum'" (p. 64). This does not mean that we have to turn our classrooms into video games with loud music and flashy graphics; as Prensky acknowledged, student engagement "depends much less on what they see than on what they do and learn" (p. 64). To solidify their understanding and engage students, we need to provide students with independent opportunities for hands-on experiences, choice, and creativity. The activities we suggest here in the area of individual instruction do just that.

The Activity: Choice Challenges

Choice Challenges is a model that can be used to generate a constrained set of activities that students can choose from as they practice or apply concepts. During a lesson, students select one of the options to complete. We suggest following these guidelines as you prepare a Choice Challenge:

1. Identify the standard or benchmark that you want to reinforce.

2. Brainstorm different ways students can practice, apply, or explore the concept identified in the standard. Consider options for using manipulatives, connecting to the world outside the classroom, and using math and science "best practice" tools and processes; also consider different modalities (e.g., visual, auditory, kinesthetic). Push yourself to create a long list. As with the whole-class brainstorming discussed earlier in this chapter, do not judge your ideas.

3. Refine your list by identifying a smaller number of activities that have a good balance among student interest, time commitment, and your ability to implement. It is not useful to select an activity that blows your budget or demands time that you do not have. When first implementing, limit the choice options to three different activities; more choices can quickly become overwhelming to both you and your students. As students become more familiar with the approach, you can provide additional choices. (Figure 3.5 provides some examples of Choice Challenges for mathematics at different grade levels and indicates each activity's correlation to the CCSS.)

4. Develop the activities by collecting materials, creating instructions, and generating examples. You should also create a short description of the activity that your students can read prior to making their choices.

FIGURE 3.5
Sample Choice Challenges

CCSS Math Standard	Choice 1	Choice 2	Choice 3
Kindergarten—Geometry Describe objects in the environment using names of shapes, and describe the relative positions of these objects using terms such as *above, below, beside, in front of, behind,* and *next to.*	Students use a digital camera or sketchbook and colored pencils to identify and name shapes in the classroom.	Students use a digital camera or sketchbook and colored pencils to identify and name shapes in picture books.	Students review a collection of pictures and use the terms (e.g., *above, below)* to describe the relation of different objects in each picture.
Grade 4—Fractions Decompose a fraction into a sum of fractions with the same denominator in more than one way, recording each decomposition by an equation. Justify decompositions, for example, by using a visual fraction model.	Students decompose fractions for a variety of visual models (e.g., a cake in 8 pieces, a container with 12 eggs, a 24-pack of soda) and record resulting equations.	Students select a card from a deck (cards printed with fractions). They use cards from a second deck, consisting of fractions that can be added in different ways, to create the fraction from the first deck.	Students use arts and crafts materials to create a visual representation of a fraction and its resulting equation.
Grade 8—Functions Describe qualitatively the functional relationship between two quantities by analyzing a graph (e.g., where the function is increasing or decreasing, linear or nonlinear). Sketch a graph that exhibits the qualitative features of a function that has been described verbally.	Students review a collection of graphs and qualitative descriptions and match each graph with its description.	Students write descriptions for a collection of graphs.	Students develop graphs to match written descriptions of two quantities.
Grade 11—Math Use data from a sample survey to estimate a population mean or proportion; develop a margin of error through the use of simulation models for random sampling.	Create and implement a survey to determine the amount of time that a sample of students in your school use social media websites each week. Create an estimate of the population mean and margin of error for your entire school.	Create and implement a survey to determine the number of text messages that a sample of students in your school send each day. Create an estimate of the population mean and margin of error for your entire school.	Create and implement a survey to determine the number of hours per week that a sample of students in your school exercise. Create an estimate of the population mean and margin of error for the entire school.

The Activity: Cosmic Comic

Bad jokes are a staple of most science teachers' repertoire. For example, Eric used to elicit groans from his students as he rattled off dozens of "Ohm jokes" throughout his lessons on electricity (e.g., "What is the name of the first electricity detective? Sherlock Ohm"). Jokes—even bad ones—can actually help students engage with content; humor positively promotes learning by focusing attention, reducing tension, personalizing content, and creating a more positive learning climate (Wandersee, 1982). Challenging students to create their own jokes or cartoons can serve a serious (and joyful) instructional purpose. Before students can invent or complete a joke, they need to have a high level of interest, a strong conceptual understanding of the material, and the ability to recognize connections between topics.

 Understanding and creating humorous jokes is a sophisticated use of language, typically requiring second-language acquisition intermediate stage fluency (approximately 3–5 years; Hill & Flynn, 2006).

To implement the Cosmic Comic activity, students do the following:

1. Identify at least two concepts from the unit that can be compared (provide scaffolding as needed, in the form of a vocabulary list or study guide).

2. Find images online or draw two characters that represent these concepts.

3. Invent dialogue for the cartoon. The dialogue should illustrate how the two concepts are similar or different.

4. Create the comic (by hand, using Word drawing tools or an online comic generator or app, e.g., ComicLife, Pixton, Comic Creator).

Another way to inject humor into the learning equation is to develop a classroom meme that continues throughout the year. You can expect your middle and high school students to be very familiar with current Internet memes (images that represent cultural ideas, symbols, or lessons; see the Know Your Meme website, http://knowyourmeme.com/)—and they are used to not only sharing these, but inventing them as well. Using this existing experience and talent in the classroom can be an effective way to engage students.

As a caution, most Internet memes skirt the edges of propriety (and many are inappropriate for school use), so select the theme carefully. In addition, popular memes change as frequently as the weather, so to be most effective, be sure to use a current meme rather than an outdated one. To implement this activity, present your own meme to the class as an introduction. Have students identify the characteristics that are being satirized in the meme and brainstorm ways that a concept from the unit might be associated with those characteristics. Then have students create their own memes (e.g., drawing, photo edit, joke).

One meme that seems to be standing the test of time is Chuck Norris, the action movie actor; he is broadly portrayed as invulnerable and all-powerful (e.g., "When Chuck Norris does a pushup, he isn't lifting himself up; he's pushing the Earth down"). A middle-school science teacher we know recently capitalized on this idea by challenging his students to create Chuck Norris memes. Student responses showed inventive use of content:

• Chuck Norris needed a trashcan. He roundhouse-kicked the fabric of space and made a black hole.

• Only Chuck Norris can enter the event horizon of a black hole and come out alive.

• Chuck Norris traveled back in time billions of years and met Mr. T. They had a battle of epic proportions. We now know that fight as the Big Bang.

As Opitz and Ford (2014) noted, combining individual instruction or independent study with whole-class discussion and review after a project is completed reinforces students' identification with the classroom as a community of learners. Incorporating student self-evaluation—specifically having them reflect on what they did well, what they learned or accomplished, what they might improve next time, and what else they want to explore—promotes ongoing learning and content mastery.

In this chapter and those that preceded it, we have discussed how Opitz and Ford's framework for joyful learning can be implemented in science and math classrooms. There may remain some questions, however, about how this approach relates to current educational initiatives. We address these issues in the following chapter.

CHAPTER 4

Using Joyful Learning to Support Education Initiatives

In working with classroom teachers, most of the "big questions" stem from concerns about alignment with policy initiatives in two areas—standards and assessment—and issues surrounding the achievement gap. One of the challenges you may face in implementing the joyful learning framework is overcoming misconceptions about what joy in learning looks like. Judy Willis (2007) noted that "too many policymakers wrongly assume that students who are laughing, interacting in groups, or being creative with art, music, or dance are not doing real academic work" (p. 1). The definition of joyful learning in math and science that we explored in Chapter 1 clearly connects to improved learning and is therefore critical for the successful enactment of many policy initiatives.

The intent of the preceding chapters was to give you a deeper understanding of why joyful learning in mathematics and science is important, what contributes to joyful learning, and how you can create joyful learning experiences with your students. We realize that you likely have many questions; in this chapter, we try to anticipate and answer some of these.

How Does Joyful Learning Correlate to Standards?

If you pay any amount of attention to the media, you have heard that the United States is facing a crisis in science and mathematics education. Our students land in the middle of the pack on international comparisons, and not enough of them are pursuing STEM careers. From a policy perspective, this is of grave concern for the future of U.S. economic security.

In addition, the U.S. science and math curriculum is often characterized as fractured, incoherent, and overburdened (Alberts, 2012; Schmidt, Wang, & McKnight, 2005). In general, our students have been exposed to many more topics per year than students in other high-performing countries. In many cases, this race through the content has trivialized math and science as a collection of algorithms and facts to be memorized, with few connections between topics or to the world outside the classroom.

We worry that this perpetual crisis and the rush through the curriculum obscures the importance of science and mathematics for every student. As mathematician James Caballero said (1989), "I advise my students to listen carefully the moment they decide to take no more mathematics courses. They might be able to hear the sound of closing doors" (p. 2). Our goal is not for every child to become a mathematician, scientist, or engineer. Focusing on joyful learning simply keeps the doors open and helps students see that science and mathematics have a place in their world and everyday lives.

We believe that because of their identification of a smaller set of core ideas, the CCSS and NGSS will allow teachers to provide more meaningful experiences as students explore concepts more deeply, identify relationships between different topics, and build connections between the content and the real world. In turn, students will become more engaged as they see the value of these concepts and become more confident in their abilities to understand mathematics and science. Both sets of standards include practices (see Chapter 3) that describe the types of things that mathematicians and scientists do. Using these practices allows students to engage in authentic science and mathematics experiences, which dovetails with the joyful learning goal of building positive learner identities.

It is important to add a word of caution about implementing CCSS and NGSS. If the standards are treated simply as checklists, our overburdened curriculum will become even more cluttered. Instead of laying these standards over what we already do, we need to engage with them as we define what to include in (and exclude from) our curriculum.

How Does Joyful Learning Support the Focus on Accountability and Assessment?

Accountability, generally enacted through standardized testing, is at the forefront of almost every education discussion. Accountability measures are increasingly tied to school, administrator, and teacher evaluations. At the same time, new large-scale tests are becoming more sophisticated and demand that our students have a much deeper understanding of mathematics and science.

Throughout this book, we have made the case that joyful learning leads to better learning. Focusing on affective factors such as interest, motivation, self-efficacy, and identity deepens students' engagement with content and improves achievement. The increased learning achieved through focusing on these factors carries over to student performance in standardized tests. A Gallup Student Poll of more than 70,000 students in 59 districts found that students who feel that they are engaged in school are twice as likely to perform better on standardized tests than a randomly selected comparison group (Lopez, 2009). The same study found that student engagement peaks during elementary school and declines throughout middle school. Singh, Granville, and Dika (2002) examined data from a randomly selected national sample of more than 3,000 8th grade students and found similar results: student attitudes, interest, and motivation toward mathematics and science influence standardized test performances in these disciplines.

How Can Joyful Learning Be Implemented Within RTI Frameworks?

Response to Intervention (RTI) is a mechanism that can be used to more accurately identify students with learning disabilities or in need of support for learning difficulties. RTI focuses on providing scaffolded support based on how students respond to research-based instructional interventions. As such, understanding RTI is important for both special education and general education teachers. In 2009, the U.S. Department of Education's Institute of Education Sciences published a review of research related to RTI in mathematics:

[RTI] begins with high-quality instruction and universal screening for all students. Whereas high-quality instruction seeks to prevent mathematics difficulties, screening allows for early detection of difficulties if they emerge. Intensive interventions are then provided to support students in need of assistance with mathematics learning. Student responses to intervention are measured to determine whether they have made adequate progress and (1) no longer need intervention, (2) continue to need some intervention, or (3) need more intensive intervention. (Gersten et al., 2009, p. 4)

High-quality universal instruction forms the base of all RTI models. The instructional approaches described in this book are well grounded in research into how children learn mathematics and science. The joyful learning framework, based on motivational generalizations and incorporating strategies in key areas based on assessment of environmental elements, aligns with the RTI recommendations from the Department of Education report (see Figure 4.1).

RTI recommendations and the joyful learning framework also meet best-practice guidelines for teaching ELLs: vocabulary and language development, guided interaction, authentic assessment, explicit instruction, meaning-based context, and integration modeling and visual representations (Alliance for Excellent Education, 2005).

How Does Joyful Learning Address Achievement Gaps?

Marzano (2003) concluded that quality of instruction is one factor that contributes to the difference in academic performance between different ethnic groups. Throughout this book, we have discussed how a focus on affective factors in education has a positive influence on student learning; this effect crosses ethnicity and cultural factors. Padrón, Waxman, and Rivera (2002) showed that social interaction, metacognition, and real-world connections provide pathways to improve science learning for Hispanic students, and similar results have been found for black students (e.g., Seiler, 2001) and American Indian students (Nelson-Barber & Trumbull, 1995).

Social interaction around vocabulary also can improve learning for ELLs (Jackson & Ash, 2012). Padrón and colleagues explained that providing

FIGURE 4.1	
Correlation of Joyful Learning Framework to RTI Recommendations	
RTI recommendation	**Joyful learning framework components**
Tier 1: Universal Instruction	
Screen students to identify those at risk for potential difficulties and provide interventions.	Assessment, supportive feedback, student self-reflection
Tiers 2 and 3: Targeted Interventions	
Material for interventions should be selected by a committee and provide in-depth treatment of content.	Deeper exploration of content; develop student interest in and perception of value of content
Teaching should be explicit and systematic, providing models of proficient problem solving, verbalizing of thought processes, feedback, and cumulative review.	Effective and supportive feedback; develop student persistence
Provide students direct instruction in problem solving that is based on common underlying structures.	Focus on increasing student perception of value of topic or process
Provide students opportunities to work with visual representations of ideas.	Use of multiple representations of content
Support students in building fluent retrieval of basic facts and concepts.	Focus on developing student confidence, self-efficacy, and mastery-goal orientation
Monitor student progress.	Effective assessment, feedback, and student self-reflection
Incorporate motivational strategies.	Develop self-efficacy, interest, and identity as learner

students with opportunities to work cooperatively allows them to discuss and defend their ideas with others. This structure encourages students to communicate with others, enhancing instructional conversations, decreasing anxiety, and developing social, academic, and communication skills.

When students do not have opportunities to participate in the development of classroom activities and when their involvement is minimized, the implicit message is that teachers do not care about their experiences or what they have to say. For this reason, students may miss out on the type of classroom discourse that encourages them to make sense of new concepts and information (Padrón et al., 2002, p.15).

The use of real-world connections to help address the achievement gap and bring joyful learning to diverse populations warrants some additional attention. Students from backgrounds that have been traditionally underrepresented in science and mathematics fields often experience a disconnect between their lives and how the content is taught in school. When working with diverse populations, our use of real-world connections needs to be culturally responsive. Incorporating students' everyday concerns, issues, and ways of knowing into our curriculum improves motivation and engagement (Ginsberg & Wlodkowski, 2000). Nelson-Barber and Trumbull (1995) suggested that a culturally responsive instructional sequence starts with real-world experience; moves to formal procedures, principles, and abstracted concepts; and returns again to real-world context. They argued that the instructional sequence should reflect a local context to allow students to enter the tasks more effectively and make the task more relevant, inviting, and motivating.

How Does Joyful Learning Influence Professional Development?

What you do matters. Joyful learning in mathematics and science for your students is dependent upon your joy in teaching these subjects. We hope that this book has provided you with a solid foundation and practical examples for rediscovering your students' joy of learning—and your joy of teaching—mathematics and science. You will need to make deliberate choices in how you approach your curriculum, your classroom environment, and the interactions you have with your students and they have with one another. The following four ideas are intended to help you get started.

Assess your level of joyful teaching. As discussed in Chapter 2, reflect on your own teaching. Think about the times when you have thoroughly enjoyed teaching your subject. What were the common features of those lessons? Can you replicate those features with different content? Next, identify a time when you really enjoyed learning mathematics and science. Why was it enjoyable? Finally, take a trip to your local library or bookstore (or visit Science Books & Film online at http://www.sbfonline.com/) and browse. What titles or topics intrigue you? Remember that one way to inspire your students as learners is to demonstrate your own interest in lifelong learning. Don't stop reading and exploring new ideas!

Inventory the materials at your school. What resources do you have available in your classroom and at your school? Do you have (or have access to) a collection of high-quality nonfiction books? Will these books help your students identify with science and math? Talk to your school librarian or principal to see if you can acquire additional resources for engaging your students in mathematics and science.

Go beyond the school walls. Undertake a STEM inventory in your community. Do you have any informal science venues in your area? Talk to scientists at your local university. They may be able to suggest resources in your area. Think vertically! Identify teachers in grade levels above or below yours and talk to them about potential cross-grade-level collaborations. A "science buddies" program benefits both the high school mentor students and their younger partners in elementary school.

Look for joy in unexpected places. Keep your eyes and ears open for interesting ways to engage your students. Have you seen a great language arts or social studies activity that could be repurposed for science or math? Could you take elements from a popular reality show and create a challenge for your students? Pop culture and the news can often spark ideas for great science and math activities. For example, one Friday afternoon Eric heard an interview with Alan Alda on NPR about helping scientists become better communicators. At the time, he didn't think too much about it. However, a few weeks later he remembered Alda's question, "What is a flame?" (see http://www.npr .org/2012/03/23/149231680/), did some background research, and turned it into an authentic activity for his students.

Mind the gap! Do you feel the gap between the station platform and the joyful learning train is too big to cross? If so, do not try to do it all at once. Use this book as a guide. Pick one change to start with. Kick it around and see where it goes. Pick a second area to focus on. Then, build from your successes.

As you consider how you will ignite joyful learning in mathematics and science for your students, keep in mind the words of author Henri Nouwen: "Joy does not simply happen to us. We have to choose joy and keep choosing it every day" (Nouwen, 2006, p. 29).

References

Achieve, Inc. (2013). *Next generation science standards*. Retrieved from http://www
.nextgenscience.org/next-generation-science-standards

Alberts, B. (2012). Trivializing science education. *Science, 335*(6066), 263.

Alliance for Excellent Education. (2005, December). *Six key strategies for teachers of English-
language learners*. Santa Cruz, CA: University of California New Teacher Center. Retrieved
from https://uteach.utexas.edu/sites/default/files/files/SixKeyStrategiesELL.pdf

Andre, T., & Widschitl, M. (2003). Interest, epistemological belief, and intentional conceptual
change. In G. M. Sinatra & P. R. Pintrich (Eds.), *Intentional conceptual change* (pp. 175–
200). Mahwah, NJ: Erlbaum.

Appleton, K. (2007). Elementary science teaching. In S. K. Abell & N. G. Lederman (Eds.), *Handbook of research on science education* (pp. 493–535). New York: Routledge.

ASCD. (2007). *The learning compact redefined: A call to action. A report of the Commission on the
Whole Child*. Alexandria, VA: Author. Retrieved from http://www.ascd.org/ASCD/pdf
/Whole%20Child/WCC%20Learning%20Compact.pdf

Bandura, A. (1986). *Social foundations of thought and action: A social cognitive theory*. Englewood
Cliffs, NJ: Prentice Hall.

Black, P., & Harrison, C. (2004). *Science inside the black box: Assessment for learning in the
science classroom*. London: GL Assessment.

Blackwell, L., Trzesniewski, K., & Dweck, C. S. (2007). Implicit theories of intelligence predict
achievement across an adolescent transition: A longitudinal study and an intervention.
Child Development, 78, 246–263. http://dx.doi.org/10.1111/j.1467-8624.2007.00995.x

Brickhouse, N. W., Lowery, P., & Schultz, K. (2000). What kind of girl does science? The
construction of school science identities. *Journal of Research in Science Teaching. 37*(5),
441–458.

Brickhouse, N. W., & Potter, J. T. (2001). Young women's scientific identity formation in an urban
context. *Journal of Research in Science Teaching. 38*, 965–980. http://dx.doi.org/10.1002
/tea.1041

Burke, P. J., & Stets, J. (2009). *Identity theory*. New York: Oxford University Press.

Caballero, J. (1989). Everybody a mathematician? *CAIP Quarterly, 2*(2), 2.

Carlone, H. B., & Johnson, A. (2007). Understanding the science experiences of successful
women of color: Science identity as an analytic lens. *Journal of Research in Science Teaching, 44*, 1187–1218. http://dx.doi.org/10.1002/tea.20237

Cho, S., Xu, Y., & Rhodes, J. A. (2010). Examining English language learners' motivation of, and engagement in reading: A qualitative study. *The Reading Matrix, 10*, 205–221.

Clark, J. C., & Groves, S. (2012). Teaching primary science: Emotions, identity and the use of practical activities. *The Australian Educational Researcher, 39*, 463–475. http://dx.doi .org/10.1007/s13384-012-0076-6

Clarkson, L. C., Robelia, B., Chahine, I., Fleming, M., & Lawrenz, F. (2007). Rulers of different colors: Inquiry into measurement. *Teaching Children Mathematics, 14*(1), 34–39.

Cobern, W. W., & Loving, C. C. (2002). Investigation of preservice elementary teachers' thinking about science. *Journal of Research in Science Teaching, 39*, 1016–1031. http://dx.doi .org/10.1002/tea.10052

Csikszentmihalyi, M., & Nakamura, J. (1989). The dynamics of intrinsic motivation: A study of adolescents. In R. Ames & C. Ames (Eds.), *Research on motivation in education: Goals and cognitions* (pp. 45–71). New York: Academic Press.

Dreher, M. J., & Voelker, A. N. (2004). Choosing informational books for primary-grade class-rooms: The importance of balance and quality. In E. W. Saul (Ed.), *Crossing borders in literacy and science instruction: Perspectives on theory and practice* (pp. 260–276). Newark, DE: International Reading Association & Arlington, VA: National Science Teachers Association.

Echevarria, J., Vogt, M. E., & Short, D. (2012). *Making content comprehensible for English learners: The SIOP model* (4th ed.). Boston: Pearson.

Fast, L. A., Lewis, J. L., Bryant, M. J., Bocian, K. A., Cardullo, R. A., Rettig, M., & Hammond, K. A. (2010). Does math self-efficacy mediate the effect of the perceived classroom environment on standardized math test performance? *Journal of Educational Psychology, 102,* 729–740. http://dx.doi.org/10.1037/a0018863

Fluckiger, J., Vigil, Y., Pasco, R., & Danielson, K. (2010). Formative feedback: Involving students as partners in assessment to enhance learning. *College Teaching, 58*(4), 136–140. http:// dx.doi.org/10.1080/87567555.2010.484031

Georghiades, P. (2000). Beyond conceptual change learning in science education: Focusing on transfer, durability and metacognition. *Educational Research, 42*, 119–139. http://dx.doi .org/10.1080/001318800363773

Gerber D. T., Hartman, D., & Brunsell, E. (2009). Mock SB&F prize election: Engaging middle school students with high quality science trade books. *Science Books & Films, 45*(2), 57–59.

Gersten, R., Beckmann, S., Clarke, B., Foegen, A., Marsh, L., Star, J. R., & Witzel, B. (2009, April). *Assisting students struggling with mathematics: Response to Intervention (RtI) for elementary and middle schools* (NCEE 2009-4060). Washington, DC: U.S. Department of Education, National Center for Education Evaluation and Regional Assistance, Institute of Education Sciences. Retrieved from http://ies.ed.gov/ncee/wwc/pdf/practice_guides/rti_math _pg_042109.pdf .

Gilbert, A., & Yerrick, R. (2001). Same school, separate worlds: A sociocultural study of identity, resistance, and negotiation in a rural, lower track science classroom. *Journal of Research in Science Teaching, 38,* 574–598. http://dx.doi.org/10.1002/tea.1019

Ginsberg, M. B., & Wlodkowski, R. J. (2000). *Creating highly motivating classrooms for all students: A schoolwide approach to powerful teaching with diverse learners*. San Francisco: Jossey-Bass.

Griffin Burns, L. (2012). *Citizen scientists: Be a part of scientific discovery from your own backyard.* New York: Holt.

Hattie, J. C. (2009). *Visible learning: A synthesis of over 800 meta-analyses relating to achievement.* London: Routledge, Taylor & Francis.

Haycock, K. (1998). Good teaching matters: How well qualified teachers can close the gap. *Thinking K–16, 3*(2), 1–14.

Hill, C., Corbett, C., & St. Rose, A. (2010). *Why so few? Women in science, technology, engineering, and mathematics* Washington, DC: American Association of University Women. Retrieved from http://www.aauw.org/files/2013/02/Why-So-Few-Women-in-Science-Technology-Engineering-and-Mathematics.pdf

Hill, J., & Flynn, K. M. (2006). *Classroom instruction that works with English language learners.* Alexandria, VA: ASCD.

Jackson, J. K., & Ash, G. (2012). Science achievement for all: Improving science performance and closing achievement gaps. *Journal of Science Teacher Education, 23,* 723–744. http://dx.doi.org/10.1007/s10972-011-9238-z

Jacobson, N. (Producer), & Freudenthal, T. (Director). (2010). *Diary of a wimpy kid.* United States: 20th Century Fox.

Jarvis, M., & Lewis, T. (2002). Art, design, & technology—A plea to reclaim the senses. *Journal of Art and Design Education, 21,* 124–131. http://dx.doi.org/10.1111/1468-5949.00307

Jones, M. G., & Carter, G. (2007). Science teacher attitudes and beliefs. In S. K. Abell & N. G. Lederman (Eds.), *Handbook of research on science education* (pp. 1067–1104). New York: Routledge.

Kane, R. G., Sandretto, S., & Heath, C. (2002). Telling half the story: A critical review of the research into tertiary teachers' beliefs. *Review of Educational Research, 72,* 177–228. http://dx.doi.org/10.3102/00346543072002177

Kann, V. (2010). *Pinkalicious: School rules!* New York: HarperCollins.

Ketelhut, D. J. (2007). The impact of student self-efficacy on scientific inquiry skills: An exploratory investigation in River City, a multi-user virtual environment. *Journal of Science Education and Technology, 16*(1), 99–111. http://dx.doi.org/10.1007/s10956-006-9038-y

Krashen, S. D. (1987). *Principles and practice in second language acquisition.* Englewood Cliffs, NJ: Prentice Hall.

Lee, O., & Fradd, S. H. (1998). Science for all, including students from non-English-language backgrounds. *Educational Researcher, 27*(4), 12–21.

Linnenbrink, E. A., & Pintrich, P. R. (2003). The role of self-efficacy beliefs in student learning and engagement in the classroom. *Reading and Writing Quarterly, 19,* 119–137. http://dx.doi.org/10.1080/10573560308223

Liu, M., Horton, L., Olmanson, J., & Toprac, P. (2011). A study of learning and motivation in a new media enriched environment for middle school science. *Educational Technology Research and Development, 59,* 249–265. http://dx.doi.org/10.1007/s11423-011-9192-7

Lopez, S. J. (2009, August). *Engagement, performance on standardized tests, and the Gallup student poll.* Retrieved from http://www.gallupstudentpoll.com/122156/engagement-performance-standardized-tests-gallup-student-poll.aspx

Lynch, S. J. (2000). *Equity and science education reform.* Mahwah, NJ: Erlbaum.

Marcarelli, K. (2010). *Teaching science with interactive notebooks.* Thousand Oaks, CA: Corwin.

Marshall, J. C. (2013). *Succeeding with inquiry in science and math classrooms.* Alexandria, VA: ASCD.

Marzano, R. J. (2003). *What works in schools: Translating research into action.* Alexandria, VA: ASCD.

Midgley, C., Feldlaufer, H., & Eccles, J. S. (1989). Change in teacher efficacy and student self- and task-related beliefs in mathematics during the transition to junior high school. *Journal of Educational Psychology, 81,* 247–258. http://dx.doi.org/10.1037/0022-0663.81.2.247

Nasir, N. S., & Saxe, G. B. (2003). Ethnic and academic identities: A cultural practice perspective on emerging tensions and their management in the lives of minority students. *Educational Researcher, 32*(5), 14–18. http://dx.doi.org/10.3102/0013189X032005014

National Governors Association Center for Best Practices, Council of Chief State School Officers. (2010). *Common Core State Standards for mathematics.* Washington, DC: Author. Retrieved from http://www.corestandards.org/the-standards

Nelson-Barber, S., & Trumbull, E. (1995). *Culturally responsive mathematics and science education for native students.* San Francisco: WestEd.

Nouwen, H. J. M. (2006). *Here and now: Living in the spirit.* New York: Crossroads Publishing.

O'Brien, V., Martinez-Pons, M., & Kopala, M. (1999). Mathematics self-efficacy, ethnic identity, gender, and career interests related to mathematics and science. *Journal of Educational Research, 92,* 231–235. http://dx.doi.org/10.1080/00220679909597600

O'Donnell, B. (2009). What effective math teachers have in common. *Teaching Children Mathematics, 16,* 118–124.

Olitsky, S. (2006). Facilitating identity formation, group membership, and learning in science classrooms: What can be learned from out-of-field teaching in an urban school? *Science Education, 91,* 201–221.

Opitz, M. F., & Ford, M. P. (2014). *Engaging minds in the classroom: The surprising power of joy.* Alexandria, VA: ASCD.

Padrón, Y. N., Waxman, H. C., & Rivera, H. H. (2002) *Educating Hispanic students: Obstacles and avenues to improved academic achievement.* Santa Cruz, CA: Center for Research on Education, Diversity & Excellence.

Pajares, F. (1996). Self-efficacy beliefs in academic settings. *Review of Educational Research, 66,* 543–578. http://dx.doi.org/10.3102/00346543066004543

Pintrich, P. R., Marx, R. W., & Boyle, R. A. (1993). Beyond cold conceptual change: The role of motivational beliefs and classroom contextual factors in the process of conceptual change. *Review of Educational Research, 63,* 167–199. http://dx.doi .org/10.3102/00346543063002167

Prensky, M. (2005). "Engage me or enrage me": What today's learners demand. *EDUCAUSE Review, 40*(5), 60–64. Retrieved from http://www.educause.edu/ero /article/"engage-me-or-enrage-me"-what-today's-learners-demand

Rantala, T., & Maatta, K. (2012). Ten theses of the joy of learning at primary schools. *Early Child Development and Care, 182*(1), 87–105. http://dx.doi.org/10.1080/03004430.2010.545124

Romance, N. R., & Vitale, M. R. (2005). *A knowledge-focused multi-part strategy for enhancing student reading comprehension proficiency in grade 5.* Paper presented at the annual meeting of the International Reading Association, San Antonio, Texas. Retrieved from http://jtscience .startlogic.com/ideas3/pubs-pres/articles-learrning-literacy/Multi-Part-Strategy.pdf

Rosebery, A., Warren, B., & Conant, F. (1992). Appropriating scientific discourse: Findings from language minority classrooms. *Journal of Learning Sciences, 2*(1), 61–94. http://dx.doi .org/10.1207/s15327809jls0201_2

Rosser, S. V. (1995). *Teaching the majority: Breaking the gender barrier in science, mathematics, and engineering.* New York: Teachers College Press.

Schmidt, J. A., Smith, M. C., & Shumow, L. (2009, October). *Science-in-the-moment. Executive summary report.* Retrieved from http://scienceinthemoment.cedu.niu.edu/scienceinthe moment/reports/SciMoExecutiveSummary_no_identifiers.final.pdf

Schmidt, W. H., Wang, H. C., & McKnight, C. C. (2005). Curriculum coherence: An examination of U.S. mathematics and science content standards from an international perspective. *Journal of Curriculum Studies, 37*(5), 525–559.

Schweinle, A., Meyer, D. K., & Turner, J. C. (2006). Striking the right balance: Students' motivation and affect in elementary mathematics. *Journal of Educational Research, 99,* 271–293. http://dx.doi.org/10.3200/JOER.99.5.271-294

Seiler, G. (2001). Reversing the "standard" direction: Science emerging from the lives of African American students. *Journal of Research in Science Teaching, 38,* 1000–1014. http://dx.doi .org/10.1002/tea.1044

Sheldon, S. (2004). *Are you afraid of the dark?* New York: Time Warner.

Singh, K., Granville, M., & Dika, S. (2002). Mathematics and science achievement: Effects of motivation, interest, and academic engagement. *Journal of Educational Research, 95*(6), 323.

Stiggins, R. J. (2005). From formative assessment to assessment for learning: A path to success in standards-based schools. *Phi Delta Kappan, 87,* 324–328. Retrieved from http://ati .pearson.com/downloads/fromformat_k0512sti1.pdf

Tough, P. (2012). *How children succeed: Grit, curiosity, and the hidden power of character.* Boston: Houghton Mifflin.

Varelas, M., & Pappas, C. C. (2006). Intertextuality in read-alouds of integrated science-literacy units in urban primary classrooms. *Cognition and Instruction, 24,* 211–259. http://dx.doi .org/10.1207/s1532690xci2402_2

Vogt, M., & Shearer, B. (2010). *Reading specialists and literacy coaches in the real world* (3rd ed.). New York: Pearson.

Wandersee, J. H. (1982). Humor as a teaching strategy. *American Biology Teacher, 44,* 212–218. http://dx.doi.org/10.2307/4447475

What Works Clearinghouse. (2012, May). *Improving mathematical problem solving in grades 4 through 8: Educator's practice guide.* Washington, DC: U.S. Department of Education, Institute of Education Sciences. Retrieved from http://ies.ed.gov/ncee/wwc/pdf/practice _guides/mps_pg_052212.pdf

Willis, J. (2007, Summer). The neuroscience of joyful education. *Educational Leadership, 64.* Retrieved from http://www.ascd.org/publications/educational-leadership/summer07/vol64 /num09/The-Neuroscience-of-Joyful-Education.aspx

Winograd, K. (1992). What fifth graders learn when they write their own math problems. *Educational Leadership, 49*(7), 64–67.

Index

Note: The letter *f* following a page number denotes a figure.

About the Authors

Eric Brunsell is associate professor of science education in the Department of Curriculum and Instruction and coordinator of the Center for Excellence in Teaching and Learning at the University of Wisconsin Oshkosh. He is a former high school science teacher and has been on the leadership team of several state and federal grant projects related to science and literacy, elementary science and mathematics, and science education leadership. Brunsell has provided professional development sessions and presentations throughout the United States and in Croatia, Egypt, Greece, Israel, Spain, and the United Arab Emirates. Brunsell may be reached at brunsele@uwosh.edu.

Michelle A. Fleming is assistant professor of science and mathematics education in the Department of Teacher Education at Wright State University in Dayton, Ohio, where she teaches undergraduate and graduate courses. Fleming is a former elementary and middle school teacher and enjoys collaborating with teachers and educational researchers across the country. She provides consulting and external program evaluation services and actively presents at local, state, national, and international conferences. Fleming is particularly interested in the equity and access issues around science and mathematics education, as well as students' and teachers' attitudes and perceptions of the nature of these disciplines. She may be contacted at michelle.fleming@wright.edu.

About the Editors

Michael F. Opitz is professor emeritus of reading education at the University of Northern Colorado, where he taught undergraduate and graduate courses. An author and literacy consultant, Michael provides inservice and staff development sessions and presents at state and international conferences and also works with elementary school teachers to plan, teach, and evaluate lessons focused on different aspects of literacy. He is the author and coauthor of numerous books, articles, and reading programs.

Michael P. Ford is chair of and professor in the Department of Literacy and Language at the University of Wisconsin Oshkosh, where he teaches undergraduate and graduate courses. He is a former Title I reading and 1st grade teacher. Michael is the author of 5 books and more than 30 articles. Michael has worked with teachers throughout the country and his work with the international school network has included staff development presentations in the Middle East, Europe, Africa, South America, and Central America.

Friends and colleagues for more than two decades, Opitz and Ford began working together as a result of their common reading education interests. Through their publications and presentations, they continue to help educators reach readers through thoughtful, purposeful instruction grounded in practical theory.

Related ASCD Resources: Engaging and Joyful Teaching and Learning in Science and Math

At the time of publication, the following ASCD resources were available (ASCD stock numbers appear in parentheses). For up-to-date information about ASCD resources, go to www.ascd.org.

ASCD EDge Group
Exchange ideas and connect with other educators interested in differentiated instruction on the social networking site ASCD EDge™ at http://ascdedge.ascd.org.

Print Products
Common Core Standards for Elementary Grades 3–5 Math & English Language Arts: A Quick-Start Guide by Amber Evenson, Monette McIver, Susan Ryan, Amitra Schwols, and John Kendall (#113015)
Common Core Standards for Elementary Grades K–2 Math & English Language Arts: A Quick-Start Guide by Amber Evenson, Monette McIver, Susan Ryan, Amitra Schwols, and John Kendall (#113014)
Common Core Standards for High School Mathematics: A Quick-Start Guide by Amitra Schwols, Kathleen Dempsey, and John Kendall (#113011)
Common Core Standards for Middle School Mathematics: A Quick-Start Guide by Amitra Schwols, Kathleen Dempsey and John Kendall (#113013)
Concept-Rich Mathematics Instruction: Building a Strong Foundation for Reasoning and Problem Solving by Meir Ben-Hur (#106008)
Curriculum 21: Essential Education for a Changing World edited by Heidi Hayes Jacobs (#109008)
Create Success!: Unlocking the Potential of Urban Students by Kadhir Rajagopal (#111022)
Creating the Opportunity to Learn: Moving from Research to Practice to Close the Achievement Gap by A. Wade Boykin and Pedro Noguera (#197157)
Engaging the Whole Child: Reflections on Best Practices in Learning, Teaching, and Leadership edited by Marge Scherer and the *Educational Leadership* Staff (#109103)
Everyday Engagement: Making Students and Parents Your Partners in Learning by Katy Ridnouer (#109009)
Exemplary Practices for Secondary Math Teachers by Alfred S. Posamentier, Daniel Jaye, and Stephen Krulik (#106005)
Priorities in Practice: The Essentials of Mathematics, Grades 7–12: Effective Curriculum, Instruction, and Assessment by Kathy Checkley (#106129)
Priorities in Practice: The Essentials of Mathematics, Grades K–6: Effective Curriculum, Instruction, and Assessment by Kathy Checkle (#106032)
Priorities in Practice: The Essentials of Science, Grades 7–12: Effective Curriculum, Instruction, and Assessment by Rick Allen (#107119)
Priorities in Practice: The Essentials of Science, Grades K–6: Effective Curriculum, Instruction, and Assessment by Rick Allen (#106206)
Succeeding with Inquiry in Science and Math Classrooms by Jeff C. Marshall (#113008)

THE WHOLE CHILD   The Whole Child Initiative helps schools and communities create learning environments that allow students to be healthy, safe, engaged, supported, and challenged. To learn more about other books and resources that relate to the whole child, visit www.wholechildeducation.org.

For more information: send e-mail to member@ascd.org; call 1-800-933-2723 or 703-578-9600, press 2; send a fax to 703-575-5400; or write to Information Services, ASCD, 1703 N. Beauregard St., Alexandria, VA 22311-1714 USA.